The Word

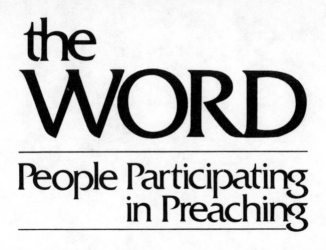

the WORD

People Participating in Preaching

MARTIN E. MARTY

FORTRESS PRESS   PHILADELPHIA

COPYRIGHT © 1984 BY FORTRESS PRESS

Library of Congress Cataloging in Publication Data

Marty, Martin E., 1928–
    The word: people participating in preaching.

    1. Preaching.   I. Title.
BV4211.2.M276 1984   251   83–16611
ISBN 0–8006–1778–9

K476I83   Printed in the United States of America   1–1778

To
Richard R. Caemmerer
Teacher-*with*

Contents

1. Preach with Me

"*Preach* to me!" Half a billion people imply that each week. They may not form those exact words on their lips. Some of them may in effect have said them only once, and then through the symbolic action of others. A committee of their Church, speaking for them, "called" someone to preach to them all. Others duplicate the meaning of the words by the position of their bodies. They have come to stand or sit in range of a Christian who is prepared to speak the message of God to them. For still others, "*Preach* to me!" is a command or a plea which needs no words. The one who speaks can read the appeal on the faces of spiritually hungry listeners.

"*Preach* to me!" This phrase demands that someone in public should proclaim the Word of God in a setting which is the church or which represents the church. The Word of God can, to be sure, also pass through the mind when a solitary believer reads the Bible. The Word of God, capital "W," is recognized whenever Jesus Christ is present in prayer and in trust. The Word of God moves from one person to another in private conversation. Any believer can be an agent of such movement. The Word thus takes many forms.

Believers usually reserve the word "preaching" for loud public activity. A form of speaking, it can also go on among the deaf through sign language. One appointed person discourses to others. When believers ask others, "*Preach* to me!" they stand in a tradition that goes back to a question asked by Paul. He was the agent of Jesus who spent much time reflecting on how to spread the saving presence of God. Paul asked:

> But how are men to call upon him in whom they have not believed? And how are they to believe in him of whom they have never heard? And how are they to hear without a preacher? And how can men preach unless they are sent?
>
> Rom. 10:14–15

Those questions still stand behind the answers believers give when they wonder how to call upon God. Belief, for them, is not an emotional tingle. Nor is it "feeling good." Believing is not the act of making up a faith. To believe in God people must hear a message, a story of what God has done and promises to do in their midst. They cannot hear a message unless there is a messenger. Someone's voice in person, over airwaves, or recorded on tape or film tells the story. Someone = a preacher. Preachers do best if they recognize that someone has sent them. Someone = God, God in Christ, God through the call of the people.

"*Preach* to me!" The people who ask someone to preach expect public speaking. A public has a partly random character. It may include people of intensity who want faith confirmed and fed by the day's preaching. They are like healthy people who know they need food just as they needed it yesterday and will welcome it tomorrow.

The same public may contain people of weak faith. They are not quite sure what the spoken Word, as spiritual food, will do for them. They have weak appetites or a sort of spiritual *anorexia nervosa,* which leads them to push food away though they know that they really need it.

At the edges of this diverse public are people who seem quite casual about it all. They are looking at the menu, or moving down a cafeteria line examining what is available. Being present before a speaker of the Word does not necessarily mean that they regard the words spoken as Word of God. Preaching is usually done in and to the church. The church is the set of people who are already called out by previous preaching. The Holy Spirit has acted through baptism and been met by their prior response. They are saying yes. It is also possible to picture that preaching can go on where not one of the people has heard preaching, been baptized, or said yes to the message. A Christian missionary like Paul at new stopping points confronted mixed audiences of curious, sometimes scornful, often hopeful people. Yet Paul as speaker was an arm, an extension of the church. Preaching, then, is an oral, public action of the church.

"*Preach* to me!" This plea asks the messenger to draw the hearers to accept the Word. That message brings what believers call "salvation." Salvation is "being right with God," becoming healthy and whole through the action of God in Christ. A new person comes to be where the old corrupt one had been. Salvation means being brought from the status of alien, the lost outsider, to adoption as a member of the family of God. Salvation means moving by God's initiative from being bound and blind to being free and seeing. Salvation stands for a move from saying no, rejecting the call of God, to accepting that call, saying yes. It means seeing one's life made open to more calls by God and more gifts of grace. Preaching intends to be

part of the act of saving. No wonder that those who are
alert to it find ways through their bodies and presence,
through their calls to others, and through their hymns,
prayers, and precise words, to say "*Preach* to me!"

Yet they may also say the same phrase with a different
accent.

"Preach *to* me!"

This form of the request or command assumes that the
speaker already knows what preaching involves. People
who bring messages, however, do not always know where
to aim them. The person who requests does know. Do
not preach *at* me, she is saying. Do not just aim your
verbal guns and blast away, hoping that the smoke and
sound will awe someone. Do not speak *above* me, using
a form of discourse aimed to impress others but missing
me and my kind altogether. You can reserve such forms
of speech for people you want to dazzle. I do not want
to be impressed. I want to be saved. I want to be moved
to action, to see my selfish self overcome, my new self
in Christ put to work.

"Preach *to* me!" There are many places where well-
intended or ill-intended words can miss the hearer. Those
who know what to ask for are saying "Do not preach
below me," either. Do not pander to my love for spiritual
gossip. Do not tantalize or titillate me by promoting what
the message of God does not offer—constant success,
money, popularity, acclaim, if only I put certain spiritual
principles to work. Do not change the message of God,
do not lower it or repackage it in order to reach that other
side of me which enjoys gaudy packages.

Preach *to* me means that you not preach *past* or *around*
or *beyond* me. In all these cases you may look out to a

public and forget what I represent. You may speak *at* those who have never heard the message and forget that some of us need building up on the basis of a faith already present. You may, at the other extreme, be clubby and talk as if everyone is a finished product, forgetting that some of us are still hounds of heaven, sniffing and searching for the first scraps and stirrings of faith. Preach *to* me means that the preachers should look into their own hearts and see what evils and doubts always have to be overcome, what graces and good gifts have to be subjects of growth and gain. If they use a good mirror they can also find a good window. A good mirror shows what the message of God can do in *any* person, in *all* persons. A good window allows for the reflecting of the same message of God to others.

Third: "Preach to *me!*" It comes down also to that. Preaching as discourse implies not only a speaker but the spoken to. The act of preaching is never complete if words are merely uttered to an empty room, in a foreign language, or by mouth to the deaf or by sign language to those who do not read signs. The act of preaching begins to complete itself when there are hearers to be reached. They begin to grasp what the message sets out to effect.

"Preach to *me!*" is the legitimate demand of each person. The demand is legitimate because even a "baby" or "primer" version of the Word makes clear that the name of the hearer is on the message. God made you and loves you. Jesus Christ is one of your kind, yet he is Other as well. When he gave himself in perfect self-abandonment and total love in death on a wooden cross-bar, he did it for you. When the Holy Spirit calls, this call is not just a gaseous whooshing through the world.

The Spirit calls someone with your name, with the cells and molecules which are distinctive to your bodily being. You are beckoned as a person whose needs do not serve as mere carbon copies of all other persons with their different needs.

"Preach to *me!*" is not the demand of baby egos in tantrums who are demanding notice. Or, we may say it is the call of the ego to a higher egotism. Jesus gave hearers a license to ask and seek and knock, to stand at the door and make a nuisance of oneself with requests and prayers that it be opened. He allowed them to be selfish as a step toward a higher selflessness, in which a person does not become absorbed in the inner life of God but becomes the agent in whom God lives, in whom Christ is formed: me!

"Preach to me!" We have presented a capsule of elements which come to us from an ancient collection of writings called the Bible. These capture us to the degree that they are faithful to those writings. Those writings are the scripts which have made possible the response of assemblies and preachers after many centuries. They do not say all that is to be said about the message of God. We can come at them in an original way and be faithful while assuming a somewhat different angle of vision. What if we change the request and sound it thus:

"Preach *with* me!" Preaching *to* me can leave me generally passive. True, the act of hearing keeps me busy. I may have to lean forward to grasp it. Yet the speaker can assume that I am a kind of antenna to grasp signals, a blotter to pick up what is spilled, a vessel into which to pour. It is clear to anyone who understands the act of communicating that more than passivity or passive activity must be involved. I may be "only" a silent hearer for eighteen minutes while someone who is prepared speaks. Preaching, however, involves both the active "I" and the "Thou." When preaching forgets the active role of the "Thou," the person addressed, the act becomes a kind of an "It," an inert thing.

"Preach *with* me!" is the cry of the calling church. It has called preachers not to represent themselves. Instead they are to speak under the impulse of all the believers, for them all, to them all. And also to *each*. The called preacher has to represent me as someone who once had to come to faith from nonfaith. I am a participant in preaching whenever the words of someone authorized to use them helps others grow, to come to new victories in a world of temptation. My growth in grace is a part of what the preacher displays through words from the Bible, which is now opened so that the ways of God can be disclosed in a new day.

"Preach *with* me!" We shall develop the notion of "preaching *with*" through the length of this book. The shelf of books for preachers is very long. The list of books for hearers is short. Have you, the reader, thought of the way the people participate in preaching? Have you considered that those who once called a preacher do not stop calling just because the first transaction may have occurred years before? Have you thought what a great part the people *may* play in weak or faulty preaching? What about the part people *must* play in preaching which works its fuller effect?

To follow up on these questions, to think about what "Preach *with* me!" means, we shall trace the act of preaching in a typical circumstance. It is not easy to

decide on what is typical. On the nearest Lord's Day—
and often on the other six days which also belong to the
Lord—the message of God is being passed on to publics
in prisons, in the name of the church and among prisoners
who can *be* church. They may be in prison "innocently,"
perhaps as political prisoners suffering under unjust re-
gimes. To them the preacher may have to whisper. Hushed
tones can pass the notice of guards. Small assemblies can
sneak under the noses of repressers in a way that cathe-
dral-sized gatherings cannot. Yet the quiet mode is effective. The prison may also include the "guilty." They
are people like all the rest of us except that they have
been arrested for acts which violate the laws of society.
To them preaching may be loud and clear, an agency of
the church spoken through the auspices of the impris-
oners. Even in that circumstance, its story may change
hearts.

What is typical? Where else are people saying, "Preach
with me"? The implied demand may be most clearly felt
in house churches. No stained glass reminds people that
this is church. The preacher may not climb a pulpit but
will lean forward from a sofa. The participants in preaching, those who are assembled, recognize their role because they are positioned the way early Christians probably were. They sit so that they cannot help but look
across a short space at the bodies and into the eyes of
the other participants. Not for them was the only view
that of the back of the head of a person one row ahead
of them in a sanctuary.

Typical preaching can go on on hillsides. Many a young
Christian hears the story and knows the call best as a
participant who inspired a preacher through her response

at a summer camp. Adults often go to retreats. In the refreshment of natural settings, they have known a communion with the speaker and with God. This communion is palpable; it shows up in the directness or fervency of the message.

We do preaching a disservice if we picture it following only one pattern. When biblical epics were the fashion in the world of movies, a film maker often found it valid to portray Jesus as a preacher. In one of these films the people from whom he came and in whose midst and for whom he was to die, were getting situated to hear the discourse that has come to us as the Sermon on the Mount. To the stereotyping movie producer, this naturally called for a mountain. Yet the careful viewer could see that this mountain was much like an outdoor church which lacked—but did not really lack—pews. People walked to their rows in neat ranks, zigzagging their way up the mountain paths as if in a reflex response to an eleven o'clock bell, a bell like one which calls to worship in the neighborhood where the film maker himself lived. Jesus then mounted a stone that looked much like a pulpit. The viewer almost expected ushers to go up and down the aisles with Sunday church bulletins or offering plates.

The Sermon on the Mount, or the other discourses of Jesus which first called the disciples to become followers, more likely occurred in very random settings. People probably sat in clumps, some of them with their backs to the speaker. From what we know about sleeping disciples while Jesus was in agony and despite the drama of the words, some of them may have dozed. Children no doubt circled a tree in distracting games until some adult hollered "hush!" in Aramaic, or whomped them in the universal sign language of a paddling across the bottom. Thoughts strayed. People came and went. There may have been little decorum and no decor. Even the imaginations of film makers become limited by what they regard as habitual.

Yet a scene that may be habitual and familiar to most readers of this book will serve as a backdrop to this exercise on "Preach *with* me!" We shall follow what it means to be people participating in preaching by tracking what may go on in a sanctuary when the church is formally gathered for worship. They are there to show thanksgiving by celebrating the Eucharist, the Lord's Supper, or to gather for some formal prayer service where a message is called for. They have in their hands service books, hymnals with orders of worship. Their congregation has agreed to use these as instruments for ordering worship. The people know theirs is not the only way to enact preaching, but they have come to recognize it as an appropriate way for them.

To focus on "ordinary" worship as the setting for preaching may be a bit of a challenge. It has less glamour than do settings in prisons or under the skies. Yet the challenge of the ordinary is practical because it may be of most help to people who routinely participate in preaching a certain way. It may be most useful, because by thinking thus about the act we may find in it what can easily be overlooked because it is part of routine. And in its own way, it may be "revelatory," for it may reveal how God can use our habitual, ordinary, ordered, and apparently routine service-booked settings to do startling, extraordinary, wonderfully chaotic, and certainly surprising things.

What credentials does this author, do "I," bring to the process? I have been called to be a preacher. For a decade in the pastorate I was called to preach at least weekly. Now in a somewhat different vocation, I still preach with some frequency. Yet it may be that all my times in the pulpit do not yet number a thousand. Through four of my five decades of conscious life I have usually been in the congregation, sometimes at the edges in prisons, not as often as I would like under skies, or on occasion in "house church" and living room settings. Most often the hearing occurred in sanctuaries on Sunday mornings or Wednesday evenings, where everything was more or less ordered. I have been moved to learn something: the message has greatest effect when it is most clear that the people with whom I am a hearer are participating in preaching. They are "preaching *with*. . . ."

You and I can join forces with each other and follow what "preaching *with* . . ." means by pursuing the course through a typical service book. We can here let the eye of the mind and memory imagine or re-create response to the act of preaching on a typical day. You may also have participated in more preaching than I. If so, as a reader or a discussant, you are an active agent, a necessary part, in a transaction that is completed only when a book like this comes to life in your mind and action.

2. The Gospel of the Lord!

"After the reading the minister may say: 'The Gospel of the Lord.'"

So reads a line in red in a book for worship which congregants hold. This is the last line they will hear before they participate in the action of preaching. "Preach *with* me!" the alert in the assembly may be thinking at this moment. Christian preaching can occur only if "The Gospel of the Lord" warrants or stands behind the ensuing discourse.

In many settings congregations will have heard three readings from the Scriptures. Then chanting or praying of a psalm may lead to a total of four scriptures, though in some forms of worship there may be fewer readings. These can come from various parts of the Bible. More often than not the First Lesson invites hearers to be part of the story of Israel. Since the word "gospel" means "good news," it can come from any place where Scripture leaps out, also in First Lessons, with goodness and newness. Goodness: God in action changes us from what we were to what we are to become. Newness: the old self is replaced with new membership in the people of God, in Christ.

A person in street clothes may step up from the congregation. Such stepping up to read the Lessons and such street clothing are marvelous symbols of the part people play in the context of preaching. Usually this person will have moved to a place of focus, where the height is right, the lighting is appropriate, the visual range is best, and the chance of good hearing is most favorable. The church is not just the place for set-aside clergy to read and speak. It is the gathering place of those who, like Israel in the old stories, are on the march or on a pilgrimage. The members have interrupted their week's walk to gather in a sacred place. There they recognize the presence of the Lord who has never left them. One of the people, someone who has helped chart their way or maybe just someone of good voice who has followed along, stands for everyone. This participant could be an assisting minister or a deacon appointed by the congregation. He may be an accountant, plumber, Ph.D., a person otherwise anonymous, a hero of faith. She may become a vehicle for the divine Word, the occasion for something to happen.

The Second Lesson used to be called the Epistle. Today, readings from the Book of Acts, which speak of the ancient church, or the Book of Revelation, which tells of the church to come, make the word "epistle," meaning "letter" (to young churches) less appropriate than before. Never mind: whether it relates to the church that was or is or is to come, whether it takes the form of letters or history or vision, this Second Lesson is also part of gospel. It announces the good plus the new, goodness plus newness. It is never complete unless it gathers up the concerns of all who participate in preaching as speaker, hearers, or actors.

The preacher may choose to speak on the day's psalm, the story of Israel in the First Lesson, or of the church in the Second. More often than not, however, the text to be opened for modern hearing comes from the final reading. This one, read in the midst of the congregation or from a raised place where the speaker can be seen and heard, properly comes at the tiptoe edge of the preaching. Usually, if properly read and heard, it arrives with such power that it all but cries out to be unfolded by the preacher as "The Gospel of the Lord!"

It is worthwhile to use a slow-action camera at this point because of the tiptoe position and aura of expectations. People who are to participate in preaching do well to pause for reflecting minutely about what goes on. This reading from Matthew, Mark, or Luke—and sometimes John—is a practice that goes on in hundreds of thousands of churches around the world. It has for almost two thousand years. Most of the time the participants expect their called person, someone set aside and sanctioned or "ordained" for the task of preaching to read this Gospel. The Christ who is present where two or three are gathered, present in the Eucharist or Lord's Supper, is present to faith through the sound waves which reach from heart to heart, voice to ear, mind to mind as the Gospel sounds out. There is no need to establish a sense of distance between the worth of the called reader and the otherwise-called baptized hearer. There is, however, a sense of distance between the world from which the Gospel comes and the world which finds the hearers as they were apart from the Gospel. Using a person especially ordained for this act can be a symbol of a special transaction.

Think about that ordained reader, who is not necessarily a person of special virtue or with the highest intelligence in the room. There may be better voices in range. Picture a reader-preacher with seminary training who is speaking in a sanctuary which that evening will be a theater. Actors who are graced enough to attend worship in the morning after a stage appearance will have had years of education in the arts of speaking. Bad diction or pronunciation from someone on stage may be upsetting to them. They may chafe at second-best sounds when the called minister reads. Yet they can shelve their critical sense, suspend their suspicions of amateurs, and allow for this climactic reading of "The Gospel of the Lord" to reach them. They may also, by the way, even be graced enough to find discreet ways of coaching the called preacher to read better in the future.

Whatever the gospeller's natural talent and equipment may be, the congregation is to notice that for this moment everything must be at its best. A tugboat may not be an ocean liner, but it can have its barnacles scraped, its hull brightly painted, its flag brisk and beckoning in the breeze. The reader today may not be gifted like eighteenth-century evangelist George Whitefield. The greatest actor of the age, David Garrick, once noted that Whitefield was eloquent: he could convert people merely by pronouncing "Mesopotamia." The modern reader may not be talented or voiced like Lawrence Olivier. It could be that an Olivier-like voice might draw awe to itself, so golden is it. The God of the gospel, who risked a hearing in the deafness of mortals and who made speech a way of indicating the divine presence, took chances on people whose tongues were symbolically touched by coals for purging of speech.

This ordinary, five-foot-something-or-other mortal, of dubiously mediocre appearance and talent steps into the midst of the congregation on a festival day, ready to speak. There may have been a procession, around a grand book which stands for the grandeur of the book to draw all eyes. Two torch or candle bearers can remind people of the day when sanctuaries were quite dark. The light then had to be brought to the book. That was practical. The flames recall that the gospel of the Lord is the good news of light. That is practically spiritual. While a choir or a congregation has been singing "The Verse," this procession has moved into the midst of all who participate in preaching. All this is as if to say: your eyes, your noses as these candlesmoke fumes rise toward heaven like incense, like evening prayer rises and you hearers all have to be summoned. Then our partnership can have full effect.

All week long there will be distractions. The words you hear in the din of those days will not be the gospel of the Lord. This hearing has to last, to grow. Other processions, impelled by commerce and love of commodity, will be milling among people at the mall. You will see other lights: traffic, emergency, flashlight, night-light, reading light, searchlight can all draw on the source of light, but they can also confuse the eye. See, now; hear, now! Let there be a fanfare. This is a climax.

Readers who are worth their salt have rehearsed the First and Second Lessons and, now, "The Gospel of the Lord." Forget Whitefield's Mesopotamia or Olivier's sonority, but do not forget the burden of this person's having prepared to read well. Good readers virtually memorize the text from which they will read in public. They have let it work on them so its phrases have had a practice workout session: now they are ready for the rest of us to hear.

And what of us, the participants? If God has given us

a companion or family who is provident enough to arrive
at worship generously early, we will also have read the
lessons in advance. If we come to worship alone, this
time before worship calls for more than the mere greeting
of other participants. It can allow for the last reading of
that Gospel section which, we have learned a week before
this, is to frame our day. In any case, we do well to have
made some acquaintance with it before the Gospel reader
voices it for us.

Printers of Sunday bulletins or inserts to hymnals now-
adays helpfully publish the readings of the day. They
have not helpfully assisted the reader or the hearers, however, if the hearing is to be done by people whose noses
are buried in the texts in the sanctuary half-light. The
people of God in such cases become like librarians of
God. As finger- and lip-movers they are so busy check-
ing up the reading with their eyes that they cannot hear,
and "faith comes by hearing." No, look, listen: this
reading is for the assembly, not for the private person in
the library carrell. This occurs for the ear, not for the
nose. Then the text can begin to work its way.

"Oh-oh!" one thinks after a few seconds. I have begun
to miss something. All this build up, and suddenly I find
I must interrupt a mental rehearsal of my grocery list.
Half-formed, it interrupted the Gospel, which was thus
half-heard. At the precise moment when the Gospel was
saving me by telling how God makes new people out of
old sinners, or does easier things like raise people from
the dead to love and life, *then* I remembered that I forgot
to set the oven timer. That child two rows away distracted
me at the moment when I could have concentrated on
the way Jesus found faith among people outside the circle

of faith, which was right where I had been, until that young rascal made noise. I have drifted again; another week is half-lost.

It is half-lost, but not lost. The listener can resume, gear in again, and rejoin the hearers. The text has a super-supply of meanings. I can miss some and not lose all. A different corner of the text, a different phrase of the reader, may be the one which can upset my complacency, interrupt my drift, help me rejoin the assembly and hear a message of life. Maybe such a phrase is so vivid that it can occupy my mind. I find myself doing my own interpretation. Already, as it were, the sermon has begun—*and I am preaching to myself!*

Fine: the Word is thus having an effect. Both the preacher and the one preached to are people for whom God cared enough to send Christ, for whom Christ cared enough to die. All is not lost. Yet I do well to rejoin the congregation mentally. Preaching to myself by interpreting the text in the midst of the reading is a private act even if it occurs in the public. Preaching is public, and I wish to preach *with* the preacher today.

"The Gospel of the Lord!"

What *is* this gospel of the Lord? The congregation has to know, in order to handle it, just as the preacher must know something of it. Saturday night in the theater the actor may have pronounced Shakespearean words more elegant than the common Greek rendered either in the common language of our day or, King James Version style, in common language of the good old days, but days gone. Yet that actor will not credibly have turned to the Saturday night audience and said, "The Gospel of the Lord!"

On Friday night some of the hearers might have been
to a Great Books Society gathering. There they may have
pored over Plato. Plato offers insights to illumine life,
guides for living, civil things. Yet it would not be appropriate for someone who has just gained a philosophical
vision to shout, "The Gospel of the Lord!" Nor does a
person say it when given good advice for the stock market
or when learning that the home team has won the game.
This is the case even though for many the Mammon of
the Stock Exchange and the Idols of the Team may stand
in the place where the Lord of the gospel is supposed to
stand, be, and move. "The Gospel of the Lord" is re-
served only for the gospel of the Lord.

One problem for participants in preaching is that what
is announced as good news may not seem new. Social
scientists, snoopers with interviews and catchy tests, have
found ways to learn which people best know the content
of Gospel stories and which ones possess some idea of
what these stories mean for their lives. Unfortunately,
they often show that a story can be worn too smooth.
Hearing it frequently can dull the hearer. They make easy
matches: "Oh, that again. That's the Good Samaritan.
Which I am. That's the publican, which I want to be.
That's the Pharisee, which, thank God, I'm not." There
is then no chance for such ho-hummed stories to take on
life. Each gathering for worship has to be a creative
exercise by those who participate in imagining the startling, the upsetting effect of a first time hearing.

The word "startle" and the follow-up word "upset"
are careful choices. "The Gospel of the Lord" is gospel
insofar as it upsets. Think about it: the picture of God in
the Gospels is upsetting. As a hearer, I looked for a world

of order, of merit, of balance. Yet the Gospel voices a song of Mary. She sings that God has "filled the hungry with good things, and the rich he has sent empty away." What will that do to our enterprise society? Will that not honor a welfare state? Or: I am upset that God is not wheeled out on stage so that finally I can see-feel-taste-touch-smell what God is. Then, one thinks, I will have no more doubts, no more need for faith. Instead, God remains hidden, absconded, a presence in the Word alone. I find it upsetting that God does not impress me with power. Instead Jesus, who is the Son and Parable of God, shows me what God is and is like when he comes in suffering and weakness, on the path to triumph. I am upset. Do I *want* to "preach with" such a message?

Strange to say, it is precisely because thoughts like these reverse my usual way of hearing and seeing things, that they can make room for the gospel to take effect. If there were processions and big books and candles, bells and organ, a cleared throat of a person wearing important-looking out-of-date robes, they were all helping set up this trick: it is not movement and book and candle, not bell and organ and eloquence, and certainly not robe that matter as *things* in the zone where the gospel is preached. They have caught my attention. Now the gospel catches me off guard. It tells what God is doing in our midst insofar as we are unimportant, not splendid, equal in need.

The odds are strong that in effective worship the reader-preacher was not the one who chose the readings. This gospel of the Lord was chosen for us. Some distant, nameless, faceless committee which planned service books or lectionaries, lists of readings, suggested or prescribed them. These texts follow a cycle through the years, or through three years, to give more variety and to help us participate in more gospel possibilities. They signal that people of other than our own loved church, people of other churches, may well be celebrating as we are, be they in Sri Lanka, Cameroun, Rome, or Finch Corners. So it has been for hundreds of years in thousands of places. Participants of many sorts bring their needs and gifts. We are not alone. We are not inventors, selfish preparers of programs to suit whims. Were we in prison, a home for the aged, a ghetto church—and perhaps we *are* in one or another of these—we would hear the same gospel of the Lord which echoes in college chapels or suburban churches.

"The Gospel of the Lord."

If I am to preach *with* the preacher I do well to think of what the gospel is not. At least it is not these four:

It is not, first, a sweet and sentimental story in which everything turns out right, one which promises me that all is well, that "Christ is the Answer" no matter what the question. The temptation to think in such terms is natural, but they rule out gospel. They eliminate my chance to preach *with* the messenger. The gospel is not necessary in a world of answers and natural wellness. The gospel comes from a world and a book in which suffering characters like Job and Habakkuk had to *keep on* asking "why?" when the plot never became clear and their suffering continued. The psalmist, who was praising from the pits, often remained in the pits. The forgiven were forgiven and maybe on the day of the chosen Gospel's event, were healed. But they also sinned again, and then died. Their dying must have led some who were left behind with guilt and tears. The pain, and the pits, are not gone yet—and they will not disappear within history, even though the gospel all but preaches itself and is read and acted upon by people.

Mark, one of the Gospels, helps me understand this. In its sixteen chapters the faithful searcher will find no moment in which the disciples received credit for having caught on to the gospel. Once, for a split second, a disciple named Peter looks or sounds good, because he is quoting someone who had the sense to see who Jesus Christ really was. A moment later all this evaporates and the words of congratulation from Jesus are forgotten. Peter must be removed from the sight of Jesus, for Peter's word is "Satan," the enemy of God. Mark's Gospel of the Lord sometimes sees Jesus congratulating outsiders or foreigners or people at the margins. Yet the disciples look half-blind, stumbling, sometimes stupid, often petty. Why? Perhaps they resist the gospel of the Lord. That gospel is the call of and to the cross, which is the last thing the disciples recognize. They want grace, but they want it cheaply. They want triumph, without walking the path to it.

"The Gospel of the Lord" according to Mark was written *after* the resurrection of Jesus. This means that those who first told, then heard, then wrote, and then preached this story, had found a new angle from which to regard the stupor of the disciples. The cross looks different after the resurrection, but it does not go away. Not when we participants need it, which means daily in life under the cross. Gospels of possibility, positive thinking, self-worth, or little-engines-that-could are not the gospel of the Lord. They all obscure or help people forget the cross. Listeners to the gospel who must preach it with their lives grasp that point fifty-two Sundays and many in-between times each year.

The gospel, second, is not the command or law of God. The Bible includes regulation and mandate, and the gospel makes sense only by reference to them. Sometimes a reading from the Gospel, even one which ends with the shout, "The Gospel of the Lord," also expresses the annihilating demand of God. Who can fulfill and live up to the Sermon on the Mount? Who has not, despite the warning of Jesus, put a hand to the plow and looked back? Who has not been among the "dead" who buried the dead instead of following Jesus? Who has not refused to leave a family for the cause? Who has not lusted? If participants in congregational preaching could have followed the demands of the Holy One, they would not have needed the gospel.

Because and though the message of the preacher is gospel, it does not hide the sacred power or the awesome, indeed the absolute demand of the law of God. Properly set in context, this demand has a positive place. If the gospel is the power of God unto salvation, the law is the power of God unto the care of the neighbor. In the context of "being saved," of course, it has no positive role at all. This law only serves to induce despair or terror because of the distance between God and the creature. In other contexts, however, it speaks for the God who orders and cares for human orders and carers. In the context of the gospel it serves to devastate any of the claims a hearer could bring, claims which would have made both the cross and the preaching of the cross unnecessary. Things become worse, only and always worse, whenever my "old self" hears what holiness expects and is and demands. I am thus driven to the gospel. There God, the same God, in a different voice and with a different hand creates something new where this oldness had been.

One cannot simply divide either the lines of "The Gospel of the Lord," which are now being read, or the minutes of the sermon into something like "ten for the law, ten for the good news"—"ten" meaning lines or minutes. Nor shall it be "eighteen for one, two for the other" nor "two for one, eighteen for the other." Like the rest of life, these approaches of God come as opposite sides of the same words and realities. They assume different proportions to meet different needs. Participants in preaching, however, have to know that the gospel of the Lord has not been heard unless they see the new creation emerge where the old self has been destroyed in the reading. The gospel read and preached may scold us and give prescriptions. In such cases the name "gospel" is only a convention. Gospel tells what God is for, or what God has done and does and will do.

The gospel, third, is not something which we participants invent. Humans make up comments on foreign affairs, book reviews, contemporary readings which may illumine the context for the gospel or which sometimes prevent Christian congregations from participating in preaching the gospel. We devise the therapies, counsels, epigrams, cute bits of advice, sage philosophies, which belong in lectures but are not sermons of the gospel of the Lord. Here is one good rule: if it seems to fit, we made it up.

The gospel is misfit. It tells of God's misfit choice of a people at the eastern end of the Mediterranean, and of the stranger choice of a rabbi from among that people. The gospel matches none of the preconceptions by letting this rabbi, sent from God, die. Whenever we fashion our own therapies, we do not expect to deal with the claim that only through someone risen from the dead do we have hope and prospect for life. We did not expect a law of life which says that the last shall be first and the first last, that life will come only through that planted grain of wheat which gives up its hold on life. Good news in the world says that big things get bigger, so what shall we do with the tiniest mustard seed, which, like the kingdom, secretly works to tower over all else? Is it therapy to learn that no bird falls to the ground without the Creator's care—if we hearers stay around to notice that birds still *do* fall to the ground? Dead. We are to draw life from thinking of that, and them?

The gospel has much to say to correct our therapies, inform our counsels, inspire epigrams, and move us beyond the cuteness of advice. It can even impart wisdom to our otherwise less sage philosophies. Yet it does all this not through a philosophy of life but through a set of active verbs which Jesus lived and passed on: go, do, hear, preach, heal, taste, love, be, die, rise, hope.

We would never have made them up. There is no way, given billions of typing monkeys and trillions of years, that some day they would randomly have typed out the story which gives life when we preach and believe it, the gospel of the Lord which we did not make up, but which makes us up. Dare I take time to let my mind wander as I hear the reading of such a message, as it is glimpsed through this week's twenty lines of reading?

The gospel of the Lord, fourth, is not a literary classic.

It has a classic character and it is literary, but we shall lose its power and we cannot participate if we place it in the literary classic slot. We may think of a classic as a work behind which we can never again go once we have become aware of it. Philosophers may remake the world of Plato and Aristotle, but they cannot wipe their slate clean: one philosopher has said that all great thought in the Western world has been "footnotes to Plato." People may live unaware of Dante and Milton and Shakespeare, but once they have become aware, they cannot get behind these. There may even be wrong people, people who are conceived of as enemies of faith, who have written classics. We may repudiate the evolutionism of Charles Darwin, the socialism of Karl Marx, the psychologism of Sigmund Freud. All of them said that faith was nothing but this or that, but never was authentic. We may repudiate such thinkers. But what these writers said came with a power which demands constant attention or refutation, once I have become aware of them. People do not take pains to refute evolutionists named Chambers, socialists named Saint-Simon, psychologists named Renouvier. Their books were not classics.

The gospel of the Lord is classic in that once its power has reached us and we have become aware of it, we must deal with it. The atheist has to counter it with some other word of power or be overwhelmed. A person who was once reached by it has to work at neglecting it, has to be spiritually benumbed, has to replace it. Think about what the gospel claims, that God who is in the process of creating the universe and people, including you, does not abandon this creation in its corruption or you in your depth, but keeps coming and asking, seeking, knocking,

at the door of *your* heart, praying to enter, not wanting
to be denied. A demand for decision comes with it. Can
one's mind safely drift while a candle-surrounded preacher
in a long robe reads more of it?

If it is classic, the gospel is also literary. Many who
choose to read the Bible in American public universities
are mindful of "separation of church and state." They
are eager to offend no one. So they choose the universal,
and thus least obviously gospelled, passages for literary
effect. They read the eroticism of the Song of Solomon,
the depression in vanity of Ecclesiastes, the universal
human character of Job, carefully selected hymns to love
by Paul in 1 Corinthians or generalized sayings by Jesus.
Ripped from context, these can be chosen for literature
classes. With careful cutting and pasting the textbooks
can hold back the gospel of the Lord from the books of
the Gospels. Then no one is saved. No one is to be saved.
Not to know of the Bible's cadences or the character of
its phrases is to be deprived of something one needs to
know about language, literature, and the power of story.
But to know these is not to know the gospel.

As literary classic the Bible is not the house of the
gospel of the Lord, nor does it invite us into rooms
which have the aura of that gospel. We cannot participate
in it as literary classic: we can only stand outside and
admire it. We only participate, we preach *with* its preachers, when invited inside. Here it is easy to forget all about
classicism. The original Greek to the classicists was called
"vulgar," of the common people. It was newspaper language style at best. The grammar was often casual. The
literary forms were unfamiliar.

Despite all this, a thoughtful person cannot say enough

for the language, grammar, and form of the gospel of the Lord in respect to the effect it would work. Analysts never tire of studying why the beatitudes in the Sermon on the Mount, the Lord's Prayer, or the parables achieve what they do. Critics tend to agree that these work because people bring certain prior understanding to them. Such scriptures come to us in settings where we want to let things happen to us. Preachers and fellow-believers who have previously begun to reach us with lives changed by the gospel help it along. We show respect by using its stories as themes in church windows, bases for hymns and organ works, proverbs on posters, impulses for dramatic action in the world. Parents, healers, missionaries who made sacrifices to paddle to our island, serve in our ghetto, or endure without compromise the complacency of our suburb, act in the gospel's name and bid us to participate now. Thus it becomes somehow plausible.

The gospel of the Lord, however, comes to us as something unfinished. Its parables startle, for in them God acts best when our ordinary ways of thinking are upset and reversed. We may continue to admire the beauty of the King James Version as a literary classic. Suddenly we begin to notice that many of the demands that we reject new translations of the gospel of the Lord come from people in literature departments, cultural antique shops, or museums of language. Most of those who speak up eloquently are likely to be people who long ago gave up being participants in preaching or believing in the gospel. Such people are of esthetic temperaments, or they are nostalgic. They could not in either case have chosen a better product about which to be enthusiastic. They may even know that one way to conjure the sacred is to use language which is strange, distant, foreign, other. These complainers need not be silenced, since one part of the believer's mind and heart never can let go of the beauties of which they speak. Yet the gospel of the Lord may also upset the sense of beauty and the style of literary convention. It may have to disrupt literature departments, be a bull in the antique religious china closet, the over-turner of museum cases. The gospel *must* startle.

"The Gospel of the Lord."

Then, what *is* it? That it is a story is the most obvious feature, one whose character we shall later explore. We recognize at once that the gospel of the Lord is a pro-claiming of how things are in the light of a story that is strange because it upsets our ordered ways. It focuses on the life of Jesus and his words and works at a remote moment in history. Yet it is not a story to be cherished by keepers of the City of the Dead, precisely because it is unfinished, because he lives and invites our partici-pation.

It is not possible to move further on what gospel is without participating in the next stages of the act of preaching. The meanings can unfold as we follow the motions and take part in the transactions of the message in the service of worship. Listen:

3. In the Name of the Father, and of the Son, and of the Holy Spirit

The Gospel procession has gone into recession, the torches are back in place, the book is moved to a new and prominent place where the text will be expounded. Or, in simpler services, the minister who has read from the preaching place moves from the Word read to the Word preached by making subtle little shifts. In a large brown book which many ministers use to understand the whole service of worship, what follows takes only a few lines:

> The Sermon is the living voice of the Gospel today. As God's appointed speaker and the chief teacher of the congregation, the pastor sheds light on the meaning of the Scriptures and shows how their message applies to the contemporary situation.*

"Not so fast!" thinks the new participant in preaching, the hearer who is also an agent of the sermon transaction. Not so fast! This brown book has other things to get across. Its authors presume that the preachers have plenty of books of many colors and qualities to promote good preaching. Yet for those who would preach *with* the preacher it is precisely this moment that has to be unpacked, stopped, spotlighted.

*Philip H. Pfatteicher and Carlos R. Messerli, *Manual on the Liturgy: Lutheran Book of Worship* (Minneapolis: Augsburg Publishing House, 1979), 221.

A school of scholarship called phenomenology teaches us to put in brackets, to [bracket] all that we bring to something we wish to observe. The observer must suspend not only prejudices and preconceptions but also the ordinary ways of looking at things that have become habitual. Then there is some chance that an activity will truly appear in a new light. Here, now, is a good moment to put on the glasses of phenomenology, to forget whatever we have remembered from the settings of past sermons, and picture afresh what occurs next.

Inevitably a bit of fidgeting and fussing follows. A careful preacher takes a moment to let us find our proper postures for the long pull ahead. If we are smart, we think we should prefer to scrunch down in a cushioned pew. If we are ready to be creatively upset, we will have gone into training by having a good night's sleep. If our ethics permit it, a cup of coffee or tea taken earlier to keep nerves tinged and bodily processes activated can help, since we cannot then fully relax. The preacher has to make room for adjustments by participants. At the preaching place we may see a nervous removal of voguish little half-spectacles, the better to promote eye contact, or it may be time for a change from close-up to distant glasses. Instinctively, the messenger may finger a worn cross on a chain. For the sake of symmetry: let it fall in the middle of the robe. Sometimes there is fiddling with lighting and sound. At other times we sense a shift of tone from the reading of "The Gospel of the Lord" to one that leads to a sense that the preacher has something of independent value to say.

The people have quieted, and the trivial transactions which may ready us to hear or may dull us by their familiarity are past. We face now what one Christian thinker called a "revelatory constellation." Things are now set as stars are lined up so that something can happen, there can be disclosure, the Word can occur in another way. Then the silence breaks. Maybe we hear:

"Grace be unto you and peace from God our Father and our Lord Jesus Christ. . . ."

Or: "Dear Friends."

Or: "Let us pray."

It is necessary here to consider whether a prayer at this point disrupts the momentum of the gospel. Some find it to be a merely pious, merely habitual act—remember that there can be wonderfully pious, marvelously habitual acts—which becomes an instrument to set a tone rather than a properly conceived prayer. A prayer may truly be in place. Various schools of thought argue about that. Most words of such prayers go unheard by the people, if the gospel of the Lord is truly ringing, and the congregation is waiting to participate in it. Yet proper prayers can also keep the momentum or impulse going; there are varieties of gifts, but the same Spirit, also in praying. Many prefer a brisk transition from the read gospel of the Lord to what the brown book called "the living voice of the Gospel today . . . [which] applies [the message] to the contemporary situation."

Following honored convention, the preacher may say, unobtrusively but with meaning, the invocation of the Trinity:

"In the name of the Father, and of the Son, and of the Holy Spirit. . . ."

The Trinity. Saint Augustine said that the name or concept of the Trinity when applied to the biblical teach-

ing of God is not adequate: it is simply better than saying
nothing, than attempting nothing. Yet at this place it is
appropriate. Ministers may make the sign of the cross
upon their own bodies or toward the congregation. Toward the congregation it is a regular act at the time of
blessing and may go unnoticed. In some contexts, to
make the sign of the cross upon oneself startles and
needs explaining. The act signals that the persons making
it recall their own baptism. Their bodies have gone through
the death and rising of Christ in baptism, and are forever
marked and sealed with that cross. To signal it now is a
reminder to oneself and to hearers that whatever these
lips may say or fail to say, whatever this body enacts in
gestures or leaves passive, whatever these eyes may burn
to reveal or let lie in apathy, is all done under the mark
of the cross. This means that it cuts across human en-
deavor, reaches us with power where we fail in weakness,
and keeps the preacher from letting that weakness turn
to despair or from letting any successes breed pride. Congregation: Why not make the sign of the cross as participants, preachers *with*? The gesture makes sense if it helps
recall baptism, body, and cross.

Yes, the sign of the cross is a good idea. A personal
story may make this vivid. In my first year of preaching
during a year of internship, when I was ready to cross a
threshold from being a hearer to being a preacher, I spoke
the message in the shadow or in the face of a pastor
emeritus who was an honored and retired senior. His
successor, my mentor, was a mature person, but I was
not. The presence of that noted old preacher was, to say
the least, intimidating.

The man was God's servant participating in my preaching, to help terrify and inspire me to do my best. The first Sunday which found me up front and him out there also found me preaching on a text in the Book of Acts.

> Now when they saw the boldness of Peter and John, and perceived that they were uneducated, common men, they wondered; and they recognized that they had been with Jesus.
>
> Acts 4:13

Here was an easy case for me to preach the gospel of the Lord. I could remind the people that they and I were "uneducated, common," since I had a year of seminary still to go and they did not all have their Ph.D.s. Yet together we could be bold, like Peter and John. And, was not its message gospel? People could look at us and see how goodness had rubbed off. They could see that we had been with Jesus.

Worship ended. The congregation filed past. The benign old pastor and his wife came by. His greeting was warm, his eyes twinkled. "That was a good start, young man. You have real gifts. It was an eloquent sermon." And then: "One problem: any modernist or unbeliever could have preached it." Knowing that "modernist" and "unbeliever" were virtually identical in his vocabulary led me to perk up. We had thereupon an appointment at his apartment on Monday night. There he unpacked his cryptic comment. It went something like this:

"You are close to the gospel, because you talked about God, about Jesus, about the disciples. You were close to the gospel because you talked about the effects of Jesus, about the ways the boldness of life can witness to his impact. Yet you forgot one thing: the cross. *Any* good teacher, not just Jesus, can exert such a strong influence that people can find boldness in those who have learned their lessons well. You told what good fellows Peter and John were, and what good guys we could be if we were also letting the influence of the teacher rub off. You were close to the gospel—and thus tragically far away from it. You did not feed any hungry souls, did not meet their proper demands or hopes. You forgot the cross.''

After a long conversation, not all of whose details inform the present point, he gave some advice which stuck. "Never look out at a congregation directly. Always plant the cross between yourselves and it, so you have to look around, or over, or under, or through it. You have no reason to be up there except for the fact that they would see the cross of Christ in your preaching action, and they would not be gathered were it not for the fact that the cross of Christ worked a new thing and brought them together.'' End of paraphrase.

No preacher, of course, can live up to that counsel, but the making of the sign of the cross is a good signal that participants in preaching, the preachers-*with*, are aware of the credentials of the person up front and the needs of those out front. If the preacher does not make the sign of the cross, or speak the invocation with it, we are free to think it.

''. . . the Father, and of the Son, and of the Holy Spirit.'' This message comes ''in the name of the Trinity.'' Lesson one in classes for prospective church members tells us that Trinity is not a word in the Bible. The early church devised it as a way of witnessing to the power of God, the Creator and Father, who comes in the weakness of the Son through the power of the promised Comforter or Breath of God. People of the covenant, in

which God was seen as One, were "Jewish" enough to
have a horror of lining up a string of gods. Yet they must
do justice to the fact that, as Paul put it, in Jesus called
the Christ "all the fulness of the godhead was pleased
to dwell" (Col. 1:19). They wanted to echo what a Gospel
saying had a centurion gasp at the foot of the cross:
"Surely this man was a Son of God." So they connect
Jesus with godhead, Creator, Father, the Trinity, into
which they creatively webbed their witness to the Spirit
as the presence-making power of God. Saint Augustine
was among those who used this notion of the Trinity,
this "doctrine," we call it, to connect it with themes that
relate to what is before us: preaching. He used analogy,
which means that there were some similarities and some
differences, some similarities-in-difference and some differences-in-similarity, to this idea: God was speaker, spoken, hearer. God speaks the creative Word, Jesus is the
Word, the Holy Spirit as hearer is agent of our partici-
pation. Here is where the notion of our preaching-*with*
as hearers has its analogy in the very picture of God
which Christians enjoy.

Such a relational doctrine is the first step in making
possible a new relation to God, to congregation, to nature,
to self. It is not as was the case of the Japanese person
to whom the Trinity was explained: "You have three
gods?" No. "Father, Son, Holy Spirit—is that not three?"
No. One. "Oh, I see," he deduced. "You are governed
by a divine committee." No, but we picture overhearing
and being part of a conversation going on within the
godhead. Thus and hence, the Trinity is the sign over
our sermons.

"In the *name*. . . ." This message is not in the name

of Reverend So and So. We participants may be listening in part because we are lured by the charisma, the eloquence, and maybe even the fame of this particular preacher. More likely we are here because we live near here, share the confession of the people who surround us, and have called this person to represent us in preaching the Word. In any case, it is not the preacher's name that convokes us. Most of us, unless we are in school or belong to sales forces, have not heard a lecture this week. We may only be attracted once or twice a year to choose to hear a secular speaker of name discourse on a topic of our favor.

The *name* which brings us together and opens the door to our participating is the name of the Trinity. The reminder before the sermon begins helps situate us. There is not time to think of it all during worship, but now we can reflect. To the Hebrews the name was not an accident. The name was never arbitrary, casual, distant. The name signaled the person, it *was* the person, it brought the power of the person to bear as a presence. The name of God is the reality of God, the beckoning of that reality, the recognizing that God is present.

We live into our names and in some measure may change the names to have them match us. A book on my shelves from the years of name-selecting for children reminded us that the persons behind the names William, Wilhelm, Willie, Will, or Bill or the persons behind the names Richard, Rich, Richie, Dick, or Dickie are very different from each other. God as "man upstairs," as "living doll," or "the old man" *is* a different reality than God revealed as parent, as savior, as one who makes holy or makes the divine present and calls us.

God the *Father*. I have just said "parent," for the moment at least bringing up the reminder that while the Bible usually says "Father," it often implies several parental roles. Here again analogy has its part: there are similarities-in-difference and differences-in-similarity between earthly fathers and the heavenly Father. The story of the Prodigal Son (or the Elder Brother, or the Waiting Father) in "The Gospel of the Lord" made that clear enough. This is not how earthly fathers naturally are. It is upsetting to see how different God naturally is from our nature, even though we are on the way to seeing that his difference is what saves us. Such is the story in which we participate. God gives birth to the people, suckles and nurtures them, and does other things female figures do. Once we are alert to all that, it is possible, our consciousness having been raised, to use in common the word "the Father" without contributing to patriarchalism or demeaning women.

We think of this God as Creator who is always in the process not of creating out of nothing (*creatio ex nihilo*) but of creating cosmos or order out of chaos (*creatio continua*). Here, now, in this act of preaching, God is taking the chaos of sounds and syllables and, through a human preacher, ordering so that God is present and we can be changed. A German scholar, Wilhelm Stählin, in a long-lost essay used a memorable phrase for this presence, memorable despite its grammatical clumsiness. When the words are invoked by faith in the believing assembly, God is present; God is *not* not-present. In worship and preaching, something really happens; it does *not* not-happen.

". . . in the name of the Son. . . ." It is the Son,

Jesus Christ, who commanded and authorized preaching
and was its greatest model or exemplar. Some preaching
furniture into which guest messengers climb startles them
with a carved-in line from the gospel of the Lord: "Sir,
we would see Jesus. . . ." Invoking the Son is a step
along the way toward "seeing Jesus," hearing the presence, participating in it.

The gospel of the Lord provides what someone has
called the memory-impressions of the early Christian
community. The church pictures this community empow-
ered and inspired by the Holy Spirit, collecting and ordering what it needed, what we need, of the story of this
Jesus in order to select what will save us. Preaching calls
us to participate in recognizing that through the prayerful
Word Jesus is present "where two or three are gathered
in his name." Again, something really happens, it does
not not happen, when the story is told, when the Word
comes alive. By what authority?

". . . and of the Holy Spirit." The preacher up front
is not to say any old thing on personal authority. This is
a place where the speaker can show what preacherly
ethics is. An oath, a vow, calls forth from all preachers
a steadfast resolve only to re-present what, by the power
of the Holy Spirit, is to be breathed as the uttering of
God. This occurs through words of one's own time, fash-
ioned for present circumstances. But the stories come
from under the care of the Holy Spirit. Holy Spirit is a
vague and difficult notion. Perhaps it is well that the
Word whistles by like the wind (wind = Spirit, says
Jesus in John 3), since we cannot grasp much except
effects. A dove? Feathers? The giver of flames? A comforter? God acting, being present? In preaching God as

Spirit provides what could not otherwise be known and uttered, in the boundaries of stories, texts, the gospel of the Lord. We are at the threshold of that preaching itself— in the name of the Father, and of the Son, and of the Holy Spirit. And now:

Smith speaks the name of the Lord; the Lord, who in his boundless mercy, has in the power of Jesus Christ, been established that a man would take on the guilt of his sin, and by the death and the Angel of Judgment ...

4. The Text for Today Is

"The Gospel of the Lord." It could be the First Lesson or Second Lesson; too seldom is it these. The act of becoming participants in the life of Israel is an element in all worship, and all Christian life. It needs reinforcing through sermons on the Hebrew Scriptures, which Christians call the Old Testament. In churches where the gospel is fresh and regularly heard, the Second Lesson, usually taken from letters to young churches, is more familiar. We have already established that both of these are "The Gospel of the Lord" or that they are supportive of it. So we can for present purposes collapse them both into the reality of gospel. The concern at this moment is for the concept of the text.

Participants in preaching, preachers-*with* are well-prepared if they know the answer to "Why *this* text?" Behind that stands the question, "What *is* the text?" People participate best in preaching where they have been informed a year, or a season, or at least a week in advance what the next text will be. There is no good way for people to walk into a sanctuary, gather in a prison, or mount a hilltop where preaching is to occur, and be ready for it if they have not first imagined what they would say to apply that text in their lives. The serious game of matching what one cried out to hear or would say with what one does hear cried out and said is a marvelous way of finding more in the text and also of finding more ways to live out its consequences.

In many Christian gatherings it is possible to know what the texts are simply by following mass-produced calendars. These reprint the Lectionary. The preacher need only say that this year the First, Second, or Gospel Lessons will set the rhythm. After one hears the Second Lesson elaborated on the Third Sunday after Pentecost, one can expect to hear elaborated and therefore one can well study the announced Second Lesson for the Fourth Sunday after Pentecost.

I do not find it in my place to insist that every year people must follow the Lectionary. If we are fortunate, we have all heard good sermon sequences on a book of the Bible such as Isaiah. If we are most fortunate, we have been guided by or have led classes on such a book and have been informed of the precise texts. These are mechanical items that need not detain us. The question of substance remains, week in, week out, of any and all texts—Why *this* text?

One answer has already been implied: so that we can prepare to participate better. A second answer has a good deal to do with the quality of sermons. The choice of the church's chosen texts from a Lectionary helps assure that a congregation will get something disciplined, fresh, not arbitrary, not something from someone whose needle is stuck in a groove. Any traveling preacher who does not follow some sort of prescribed Lectionary texts can report how tempting it is to have what ministers call a barrel. At the top of the barrel will be the really scintillating and clever sermons, the ones which produce compliments and inform the preachers of them how good they are. Those that are less effective, those which bombed, can fall to the bottom of the barrel.

Not all preachers travel. Those who stay home cannot create a barrel since there is always the chance that some hearer will remember something from a message preached six years before. In the congregation there is no luxury of repetition, for preacher and preachers-*with* remain near each other for some years. [This, in an important aside, is also the place for a preacher-turned-professor to remind congregations that regular preachers are under great stress. They have heavy demands on their imagination. Professors, who cycle passing classes of students, can quite easily in their weakness or weariness get away with a barrel full of old lecture notes. Preachers fifty-two and more times a year speak to many of the same people they face each year. The preachers have plundered resource books for ideas. They grow weary and need the stimulus of workshops, retreats, sabbaticals, and even, best of all, vacations, for refreshment and for the participating congregation's own good. Amen.]

Admittedly, not always will the text be appropriate to the day, though surprisingly they almost always will speak to situations. It may be that one must improvise a choice for a cornerstone laying, a celebration of some milestone in the lives of the people, or whatever. Yet by serendipity and because of the scope of the gospel of the Lord it is likely that the prescribed texts will apply. The congregation is protected not only from barrels but from book reviews, hobbies, old war horses, overdone causes, obsessions, ruts, or posings of expertise by preachers whose competence is not necessarily the economy or the foreign policy—unless it be the economy of God and the divine policy to us who were by nature foreign to his claim.

The discipline of following the theme of texts is helpful. The temptation is always strong for the preacher to reach too often for the formed topic of the times. In the years after August 6, 1945, the atom bomb became an early obsessive theme for sermons. Weary congregants heard easy, automatic, and superficial reference to the atom bomb as the all-purpose relevant theme. Once to escape this a couple decided to practice their German by hearing a sermon by an aged pastor in a congregation which still evoked by dawn's early light a German-language gathering. Only moments after the greeting "*Liebe Freunde*" they were startled to hear across the generation gap in the world of seniors the incantation of syllables, "*atomische Bombe*. . . ."

In the times of horror which follow assassinations, the times of chaos which come with revolution, the times of temptation to pride which come with harvest or victory, people are better off with the text that reaches across the ages and is spoken on the same day in nations where there has not been an assassination, in overordered countries, or where there is famine or defeat. The imposed Lectionary text is more likely to control Christians and thus bring God's power as opposed to a choice of topics which exalt human pride. For those who are preachers-*with* all this may add up to some counsel. If now and then we feel that preaching may be tired because the texts are biblical and therefore familiar, and hence we are seeking freshness by escaping the ordering of texts or going beyond the Bible for themes, it is wise to consider the alternatives. The chances are we will do better with the preset texts.

All this attention to why *this* text needs backing in what could be a prior question: why *the* text? Why any

text at all? Why not have the preachers up front spin out
their own principles and philosophies, since congregations
can live by principles and philosophies. After appraising
the long history of effective preaching one safely concludes that a textless sermon is a contradiction in terms.
A textless sermon is a lecture. Those of us who move
regularly from pulpit to podium, and who from both
locales speak on spiritual themes, are sometimes asked
what is the difference between a sermon and a lecture.
One not entirely cute answer could be to say that a sermon
as a message of God begins with and works itself completely out of a biblical text. A lecture begins anywhere
and works itself out and then may close with a biblical
text. It remains a lecture.

The preachers-*with* may at times chafe in the presence
of this notion. Some readers of the Saturday newspaper
may be drawn to clever titles or grabbing topics advertised
on the church page. Over against them it seems singularly
undramatic to say that a sermon will deal with, say, Luke
7:1–10. No one has passed legislation that prohibits
preachers from seeking to attract people with a tantalizing
title. Yet the clever theme or title is likely to remain in
isolation and never be matched with the substance to
which it refers. The text-based sermon surprisingly comes
alive more often when we reflect on the text and keep
coming back to it.

Of course, there can be such a thing as an effective
spiritual message which reports on one's self-invented
language of prayer or meditation. Of course, one can
speak as a Christian to Christians without having everything grow out of a biblical text. There is no reason to
judge people who occasionally choose such a mode of

discourse. Yet what comes forth then is such a different transaction that for the minority who favors it we say: there can be legitimate books on that legitimate theme. This is not that book. To put it a bit more carpingly and judgmentally: an attempt to achieve what a well-expounded biblical text could work in a congregation *without* a text is usually a flawed gesture. Congregations can be entertained by it, but hearts are ordinarily moved only to the extent that at least indirectly sermons derive from a biblical text, the gospel of the Lord.

Having said all that, it is now just as urgent to say a cautionary word about texts and the text. It focuses in a warning against any idolatry of the physical object of the printed text or the idolatry of a preacher's interpretation of it. Texts are made up of molecules of chemical substances called ink imposed on molecules of wood pulp turned to paper. They are likely to be black on white, bordered in white, bound within covers as a book, leather-bound and gilt-edged to indicate sacredness and importance. The object called the Bible becomes adorable. Preaching the text can mean waving the physical object of the book, shouting, "the Bible says," or "the Lord says," and claiming to represent the whole counsel of God in the name of one's own opinions.

The physical object called a text is not worthless. Try to afford a Gutenberg Bible. Mourn the loss of grandfather's Bible in a fire. Cherish the Bible you carried down the aisle under a spray of flowers on wedding day. Caress the brass-covered New Testament which stopped a breastward bound bullet in war time. Recognize the role of the book in archives and libraries. Know that people can stumble upon the Bible and be converted by a reading, as one can read the Koran or Upanishads and turn Muslim or Hindu. It happens. It happens chiefly because the people who placed the Gideon Bible in the hotel room showed their care for the spreading of the story. Most people who claim to have been converted by a mere reading are likely to have been preconditioned by exposure to the figure of Jesus as someone told about him—or lived him. The Bible in the hotel room also is a marvelous instrument for confirming what the Word in the congregation has implanted. There are exceptions to every rule.

But, the *rule* is that "faith comes by hearing." People were called to Israel before there was a library called the Hebrew Scriptures or Bible. The early Christian circle of believers in Jesus did not become believers because they possessed the most lavish and cherished scrolls with words on them. They became believers because people with names like Barnabas were good characters, full of the quality of the Holy Spirit, speakers who asked others to participate with them in the gospel. Hence many believed. Worship today is not *only* the reading of "The Gospel of the Lord," or the candle lighting, or kissing of a book called the text.

If the mass of people are tempted to idolize the text as book or page, certain scholars can idolize the *idea* of text. Texts can be very beguiling. What do scholars in the humanities have to work with other than texts? They can cherish these the way baseball pitchers fondle baseballs, scientists enjoy computers or test tubes, artists like paint, or actors like greasepaint. They are tools of the trade. The texts lie there waiting for scholarly dissection. The Society for Biblical Literature can appoint a task

force of a score of people who will spend years studying
the text of Mark 13. They can do formal or structural
analyses of how texts get put together or taken apart.
They can give lectures on all of this and not be anywhere
close to what the text is supposed to achieve as the Gospel
of the Lord. It can in fact become opaque, an icon,
something which blocks the transparency that a biblical
text through preaching can become to the presence and
power of God. Why does all this matter?

The text is an instrument, something to be used. The
text, even a sacred, scriptural, inspired text, is a means
toward something else: toward "being saved," experi-
encing the presence of God, or redirecting one's life in
the way of Jesus Christ. The preacher lives under and
with the text, and opens it for the preachers-*with* who
make up the hearing and then the acting group. When
the preacher announces "the text for the day" and either
reminds hearers that it is the gospel of the Lord just heard,
or another Lesson, people have certain needs and expectations. This is the moment to reflect on what is involved.

The first thing to notice positively about a text is that
in some ways it is a story, reflects a story, or is part of
a story. In the case of the excerpts from the Gospels it
may very well be a little story out of the record of Jesus,
or a story—usually one called a parable—that Jesus told.
Now it is a very strange thing that we who participate
with preachers spend so much of our life dealing with
stories. This is the time once again to put on the spectacles
of the phenomenologist and look at this theme as if we
had never heard of it before.

Picture a tombstone on which is inscribed a word something like this: "Reverend Christian—Storyteller." That

seems like a strange condensation of the life of a preacher. Reverend Christian may have told stories well. Like the great rabbis, "reverends" often acquire the art of spinning yarns or telling fables. Yet what ministers of our acquaintance want their lives summarized that way? What about being an administrator, parent, someone with a good pastoral way, a theologian—but storyteller? Jewish comedian Myron Cohen was a storyteller, as were Will Rogers and Mark Twain. Their profession is honest, but it seems comparatively trivial. Does the nation need a half million entertaining storytellers?

Whatever preachers have to talk about comes from a narrative flow in the story of Israel and the followers of Jesus. If one of the members of their congregation is sick, unless they are medical missionaries or they moonlight as nurses, the preachers have no potions or herbs to bring, no exercises to prescribe. They heal by telling a story, by asking the sick to become part of a story. At the point of death people want words in the form of prayers which reflect stories of a Good Shepherd or the one who healed a person by forgiving him after friends tore open a roof to get him to Jesus.

When a preacherly counselor counsels people, what goes on but, again, the telling of a story? Of course, a Christian counselor learns the techniques of advising. There must be attention to the art of listening, awareness of psychological theory, experience that comes with common sense. But insofar as the counseling person is approached specifically as a Christian, the credentials come from the common involvement of the seeker and the sought in a story. What comes out may not take the form of a story, but it implies the story which unites the two.

A story: Some years ago I lectured in Canada on what difference it made being an historian when it came to Christian faith and what Christian faith did to make a difference to the historian. After the lecture an informed person in the audience said: "Historians tell stories. You are a Christian historian who tells Christian stories. Why devote your life to that?" I answered, "Because stories 'save!'" The questioner came back, unfortunately, for I was running to the limits of knowledge: "How and why do stories save?"

Whole schools of literary scholarship now devote careers to providing technical answers to such questions. In some respects the power of story is a mystery and we do not understand its hold. To be lifted out of one's own world into the flow of another person's or people's time and place is, in a way, saving. Engagement with a story can provide us with an enchantment or magic that has a healing effect. An old Jewish story from the world of the Hasidim, the ecstatic Jews of eastern Europe, illustrates this energizing aspect of stories and hints at their saving power. Martin Buber told it and set it in a context that says something about why persons have to open texts in sermons:

> The story is itself an event and has the quality of a sacred action. . . . It is more than a reflection—the sacred essence to which it bears witness continues to live in it. The wonder that is narrated becomes powerful once more. . . . A rabbi, whose grandfather had been a pupil of Baal Shem Tov, was once asked to tell a story. "A story ought to be told," he said, "so that it is itself a help," and his story was this. "My grandfather was paralysed. Once he was asked to tell a story about his teacher and he told how the holy Baal Shem Tov used to jump and dance when he was praying.

My grandfather stood up while he was telling the story and the story carried him away so much that he had to jump and dance to show how the master had done it. For that moment, he was healed. This is how stories ought to be told.''*

Today most who are preachers-*with* the preacher up front have been taught to be sedate and mannered; decorum has become important. Yet this understanding of the text as story to be told and expounded is a clue to the reason some revivalist audiences have sung, ''I can't sit down!'' The standing, the gestures, the power of the voice of the preacher are all themselves reminders that a story is being presently enacted.

Another way to think of story is in the context of loving, for the gospel of the Lord is a story of loving and love. When two people are attracted to each other and begin to fall in love, they—do what? They do not ordinarily sit down and discuss their philosophies of life, though such outlooks are at stake. They do not exchange engraved scrolls with principles for action on them, though some of the cards they send each other might have sayings on them. No, in the long evenings on the porch swing or car seat or over dinners in fine restaurants, they compare notes. Most of this comparing is in the form of telling their stories, so that they can build trust.

''Me. Oh, I guess I'd better tell you that I was an abused child. I think I've overcome the effects, but you know that child abuse is sometimes seen as a kind of inherited disease. So I'd better tell you about the abuse

*Quoted in Johann Baptist Metz and Jean-Pierre Jossua, *The Crisis of Religious Language* (New York: Herder and Herder, 1973), 86ff.

I suffered. In fact, my father pushed himself on me in-
cestuously, and you'd better hear *that* story, too, because
counselors tell us it can color our future sexual relations. . . ."

"As for me, well, I guess I had a happy childhood. I
was attached to my mother especially, since father was
in the military. We moved around a good deal, so I never
knew my relatives. Mine is a story of quick pickup and
drop of friends. I was not able to establish any profound
relations. Let me tell you about the one time previously
I fell in love. It's a long story, but it says something
about what we can expect of each other. . . ."

Six months later, unprompted, to their surprise, if they
would think about it the two will not have begun to weary
of telling or hearing stories. None of the narratives can
be too trivial to inform or help bond the couple. Few of
them can be so overwhelming that they stifle the love
which is growing.

"Me?" asks the preacher. "Oh, I guess I'd better tell
you that whatever abuse I suffered was inflicted by myself, since I was wracked by guilt. But let me tell you
the story of how an old man helped me work past it by
the way he embodied Jesus. . . ." Or: "You?" asks
the preacher. "I guess I'd do well to tell you the story
of a black South African preacher who is this day suffering something which will bring our own congregation's travail into a new context. It happens that. . . ."
Or: "We?" asks the preacher. "It would be best if we
tried to rise above our petty and ordinary ways of thinking
by hearing how Jesus overturned everything one day when
he startled an audience by saying. . . ."

Stories heal and save.

Second, stories provide traces of events that are past and make it possible for them to live again in new forms. The gospel of the Lord includes and grows out of the story of Israel on its long march in exodus or its long departure in exile. It centers in an event that happened on the executioner's hill near Jerusalem in a story of long ago that I have to tell you now. So go sermons. Without the story, what would we have? Christians believe that they do not naturally now belong to God, not since they have been severed, by their own fault and by their participating in a fallen humanity. They do not believe that they have a natural union with God at God's level. They do not believe they can make up a religion through the plot of a saving story. They do believe that events which occurred to Israel and in Jerusalem ask of them a wager on which they are to pin all their hopes, a goal for their entire pilgrimage to eternity.

Yet how shall they hear if there be no preacher? And how shall they hear anything worthwhile if the preacher has no access to those events? And the only access they have is through the remaining traces. A wall of a temple here, and a monument there? They do not "save." At best they do no more than confirm a story. Suppose the controversial Shroud of Turin were found to have come from the time of Jesus. It would mean nothing at all unless someone knew the story which inspires curiosity over it in the first place: a story which would explain why to look for the imprint of nail and spear wounds, the marks of a crown of thorns.

All events of the past are gone. They only may leave traces. For the preacher those that count are not temple walls, monuments, or pieces of linen, but stories of the living encounter which occurred where these traces were left. The story itself is the best trace. In a sense it tries to recapture and re-enact something of what went before. If someone—Israel, Jesus, the martyrs and saints, the doubters and imprisoned—suffered and we fail ever to tell the story we come to dishonor suffering and to be less humane than otherwise. We are almost certain not to be aware of the cost of discipleship, the measure of faith active in love.

Scholar Clifford Geertz has described religion as a system of symbols—translate that here to story—which, whatever else it does, clothes certain conceptions with "an aura of factuality." They become more real than the real world around us. The landscape of Israel becomes part of the landscape of the mind, more vivid when the heart comes to faith than is the set of symbols of commerce outside the church window. One becomes a part of the story of Israel enough to learn, for example, about the role of the sacrificial lamb. Thus one understands why, for people who came to faith then and who are confronted by the story now, Jesus is the Lamb of God who takes away the sin of the world.

People tell the story of Jesus' suffering not because they are sadists who enjoy stories of violence. It is possible to tell the story of the crucifixion without dwelling on the extent and means of physical suffering. In a cruelly trivial way, we can even say that Jesus did not suffer *all that much* physically. There have to be people today suffering from cancer, and there were other crucifixion victims in his time who suffered more physically. But his suffering had special meaning because of the story of which Jesus is a part. Who it was that was suffering, the

Holy One of God, made all the difference. This makes his story more real than the world of criminals being executed in our time. When people tell the story of who this Lamb is, what the event means, they are not merely living with traces of the event. The power of the event itself comes alive now. God who was involved then enacts healing and saves now.

The text, in a way, retains and congeals the story which is itself a trace of past events. What would happen were there no text? Perhaps as children we have all played the game of telephone in which, say, twenty children sit in a circle. The first one is instructed to whisper some sort of phrase into the ear of the next: "Elephants dance well." She whispers it to the next. By the fourth something has begun to be slightly compromised, lost: "Elephants' dance hall." By the eighth, "Ellen's pants are in the hall." By child number twenty there is no trace of what the phrase first signified.

In contrast, think of writing: "Elephants dance well." Pass it on. The twentieth child can read the note and expound whatever meaning she finds in it. Of course, *that* meaning will have little "saving" impact because it is trivial. It will have importance to someone who is the child of a circus performer who may someday have to dance with an elephant. She will want to know that elephants can have rhythm and will not step on toes. Otherwise, it is a remote story, useless.

The story of a lamb and of a crucifixion would also be entirely beyond our range unless the circle out of which its teller comes is or can be made to be one of us. One reason why in the church people tell story upon story and expound text upon text is so that the repertory of themes grows. Believers have even more on which to build, on which to hook their imaginations. Now it is possible to see how a story is part of a community.

Here again it is valuable to think about what texts mean and how they mean it. Today literary theorists debate the whole notion of texts. Among many schools of thought three stand out. One pins everything on the *author*. An author-based reading of the text would call the preacher to say nothing unless something definite can be known about the mind of the author. That is most difficult to do with biblical stories because the very name of the author usually is not known. Even the most conservative biblical scholars do not believe that all the Psalms came from King David. No one knows who wrote them, in what circumstances, or always toward what goals. Suppose readers know that "Mark" wrote Mark. Do they know enough about Mark from the Gospels to gain much understanding?

To push the point further: It is possible to exchange letters with someone for many years and still not know them well enough to interpret the texts from the author's viewpoint. "Oh, did I say *that*?" a husband of forty years says to his wife when he comes home and explains a phrase she misunderstood from a letter he wrote overseas. "Surely you did not think I meant *that*?" is another exclaiming question passed between friends of fifty years. "I really don't know *what* I meant to say or intended with that phrase!" says someone who has lived with herself sixty years and thought she knew her own mind.

It does help to know as much as possible about an author. Many listeners never tire of learning what history and archaeology can tell about the world of Paul so that his letters mean more. Some sorts of connections do exist between our knowledge of the psychology of an author and what he or she conveys to us. But not enough. The author-based approach alone does not serve well.

Another school of thought turns everything around and in a phrase that has much meaning for preaching says it all depends upon the *readers*. A text then has no single meaning for everyone. In a sense, there are as many texts as there are readers or hearers to interpret it. Certainly a preacher knows something about that problem. A preacher who becomes eloquent about the wonders of God as Father will not get through to a child who knows the word "father" only as a code for a big, brutish, alcoholic person who comes home at odd hours, fights with mother, and whips him. A preacher who without explanation tells the wonders of Jesus to a collection of Holocaust survivors whose guards were German Catholics and Protestants who carried pictures of Jesus will find a much different set of hearers of a text than will a preacher who talks to children in a benign Sunday school circle.

We can test the power of this reader-based understanding of texts by instances in our own lives. We participate in preaching in different ways at different times. In one stage of life we are uncertain, and we need a story that gives us confidence. At another stage we are bored, and we bring understandings to texts that have to be upset by startling turns of story. At still another stage we have settled down into pride and cocksureness, and have become different persons than we were when we first heard the story that earlier inspired trust in the time of our weakness. Meanwhile, we may sit next to a person who is bored when we are eager, proud when we are shy, humble when we are cocksure. Next to her is another. . . .

Those who make much, too much, of the reader-based theory cannot conceive of a congregation. There is simply too much diversity in any vital gathering. The result is a form of relativism. Texts do not then mean anything because they mean everything. Each story we bring changes the story we hear. The preacher is reduced to just talking, while each of us is making up meanings, if we listen at all.

A third approach does not solve everything but it begins to explain how and why Christian congregations are formed. Between and beyond author-based and reader-based understandings of texts, there are *community-based* understandings. A Jew hears the stories of Israel differently than does a Christian, even if they both agree on who the authors are and even if they are in similar stages or situations of life—young and scared, mature and proud, old and scared again. One belongs to a community which looks for the redemption of the world: the Messiah will come. This notion colors every story. The Christian interprets texts in the light of a redemption which, she believes, has come in Jesus. Every story acquires a new color henceforth.

Within the Christian community, there has grown a canon of scripture, a rule which helped determine which texts are to be a basis for the story for the whole church. Yet even so, there are canons within canons. Some believers look to the biblical laws by which to live and others to the gospel which makes it possible for them to live. Some favor the Gospel stories while others take their meanings from the writings of Paul. Millions favor the vision stories in Ezekiel, Daniel, and Revelation. Others find them not to be very reliable as literal accounts of anything. Baptist and Catholic communities read the same texts about baptism and come up with different understandings about when and how to baptize whom: Infants, by sprinkling, as sacrament? Or adults, by immersion, as act of faith?

Perhaps I should not have brought up such an unsettling issue as the one about community understandings. By itself it does not help us much with the question of the truth of a story in objective terms. Yet we can leave that truth question for other writers, in other books, on other days. Before us now is the understanding that when a preacher says ''the text for today is . . .'' there can be a great deal of understanding in advance about why the story of Israel and of Jesus means or should mean something. Not every day must Lamb and cross, bread and wine, be explained from scratch. The proclamation that God is Creator, Father, one who loves, one who sends— all that becomes part of the canon and code of the community which interprets.

What we have just approached is one of the most difficult and yet necessary elements in coming to terms with what it is to take a text and open it for a congregation. We might as well set the technical term on the table and wrestle with it. Scholars who used to talk about interpretation, after the name *Interpres*, who was the being who served as messenger of the gods, now often speak about hermeneutics, after *Hermes*, better known as Mercury, the wing-footed messenger between divine beings and mortals. Of course, these experts can continue to speak about interpretation, but for a variety of reasons they make special points—and perhaps sound wiser and deeper—by referring to hermeneutics. It pays us to linger for a moment to see something of what is at stake in this issue.

A master of author-based interpretation, E. D. Hirsch, Jr., in a journal article* gave one of the most apt summaries of what is at stake when a preacher says "the text for today is . . ." and expounds it. All knowledge, Hirsch says, involves some form and amount of pre-knowledge. People make sense of nothing unless they bring some prior sense. "Heavenly Father" is merely a set of syllables unless they can connect something with "heaven" and "father." What they connect depends upon their personal backgrounds.

The idea of pre-understanding is crucial. At once, it is obvious that readers are moving in circles. From where do those pre-understandings and earlier senses come? Hearers encounter words and clauses ("Lamb," "Lamb of God," "cross") which do not have meanings for an audience until it sees what part they play in "the text for today." Hirsch gets complicated: "But we can only know the whole meaning through the various parts of the text," in this case the separate parables in little chunks of the whole Bible,

> and since we cannot know what the parts mean or how they work together before we know the whole text, we find ourselves in a logical puzzle, a circularity. This is the famous 'hermeneutic circle.' It can be broken only by resolving the question of which came first, the chicken or the egg, the whole or the part. By general agreement, from which there has been virtually no dissent, the question of priority is decided in favor of the whole. The whole must be known in some fashion before we know the part. For how can I know that I am seeing a nose unless I first know that I am seeing the face? And from the doctrine of the

*"Carnal Knowledge," in *New York Review of Books* (June 14, 1979), 18.

priority of the whole came the doctrine of pre-understanding. Since we know the whole before the part, we must assume some kind of pre-understanding in all interpretations.

Now it is possible to begin to see why preaching involves participants, preachers-*with*, and why the pre-understandings they bring from within their community or its margins make it possible for the "text for today," the little part of the big story, to make sense here and now.

'Twas brillig, and the slithy toves
    Did gyre and gimble in the wabe;
All mimsy were the borogoves,
    And the mome raths outgrabe.

There is another text. It is made up of molecules of ink imposed on molecules of paper. In its own way it is in English. How expound it? How let it relate to the story of our lives? The problem is that brillig slithy toves gimble wabe mimsy borogoves mome raths outgrabe do not connect with any pre-understandings. They are nonsense words, or jabberwocky, as author Lewis Carroll called them. To know that they are nonsense helps us begin to make some sense, but never much.

Where do believers acquire the pre-understandings that make possible a Christian sermon? Where do the "faces" of the whole come from to make possible our handling of the "noses" of the part each Sunday? They come from parents and pastors, trusted friends and teachers, Pauls and Barnabases, who have already won confidence in the church. They passed on a way of life and then a story to inform it. Hearers become ready to be "saved." Faith has already been worked in many of them from baptism, and now it is to be built upon.

"The text for today. . . ." Now that we are beginning to be at home with Hermes, who brings meanings between two orders of being, the divine and the human, let us put him, or hermeneutical theory, to a bit more work. I know as I write it that hermeneutics is a forbidding word on the page, and I am tempted to find a substitute. But by now there are reasons for us to understand enough to push it a step further. As with all other theories from our time, I would not press this as a final word for catching on to what occurs when a preacher opens a text. These words will pass, to be replaced by other theories in a future day, just as last Sunday's sermon will be partly replaced by what hearers have learned and needed this week. Yet we can seize from what is current one notion that informs this difficult point: Why should a person who usually wears street clothes and talks no better than anyone else put on robes on a special day, mount a high place, turn to sometimes smarter people, diverse people, and start talking to them about a story in "the text for today"?

In this school of thought, there are three angles from which to come to a text. Scholars base them on the three tenses, past, present, and future or relate them to three prepositions: behind, of, and before or in front of.

The preacher who announces the text for the day knows a great deal about the world *behind* the text, its *past* tense. One can never know too much about that world. Happy is the congregation whose preacher lives toward the text the way Samuel Johnson thought of things: "All knowledge is of itself of some value. There is nothing

so minute or inconsiderable, that I would not rather know
it than not.'' Unhappy is the congregation whose preacher
lives only toward the text that way. Such is the way of
information, of book knowledge. In the Christian faith,
however, it matters not so much what you know as Who
you know. Scholarship of a text will not necessarily bring
one closer to the presence of God. To know Christ, said
a church reformer, is chiefly to know his benefits.

Still, knowledge of the world behind the text can always inform the understanding of a text. Preachers and
hearers cannot know too much about the language, the
original thought forms, the world from which the phrases
came, the landscape. Whatever is known about Israel,
Judea, the stones of Jerusalem, the understanding of water
pot, informs. Yet after one is done with history, or with
historical criticism, the text does not come to life.

So experts turn us to a second phrase, literary criticism.
This is, in a sense, the *present* tense version, the world
of the text. In its spirit people pack and unpack texts,
dissect them, take them apart and put them together as
if under microscopes. They thus learn the function of
phrases. It is also important to know what is poetry or
prose, why authors employ images and metaphors. Not
to understand the form of a parable is to miss what a
parable meant to those who first heard it or what it can
mean now. Literary criticism, the world of a text, can
offer something to be admired, something beautiful, and
intellectually satisfying. Congregations, however, expect
more if they are to help the preacher reach them.

The third approach, says this school of scholars, has
the most promise. In a sense it is *futuristic*. It deals with
the world *in front of* the text, the world of horizons.

While the point can be put many ways, this is a convenient one: when one approaches a profound classical text, especially one which claims to be sacred, one which opens on a horizon that goes beyond our ordinary, practical, mundane world, something new can occur.

The world in front of the text discloses to us ways of living, being, and thinking which we might otherwise not have considered to be possible ways for us. Every biblical text in a way does this. We have already suggested that people are saved by a story they could not have made up. Without the story, preserved in the texts, they would have no trace of the events which disclose God's own life to them. Without this story, there would be no reason for anyone to trust in Jesus, a figure of 2,000 years ago—or to believe that this crucified One is risen. An ancient preserved text urges readers to trust God no matter what. Nothing shall separate us from the love of God—including death. Millions of Christians entertain, yes, embrace, the possibility that love is stronger than death. They do this not because they thought the notion up, or because things in the world reinforce the notion. Death looks deadly, final, antilove. People also do not think in these terms because natural science or philosophy tell them this. They consider the possibility because their pre-understandings of the whole story of Christian faith lead them to understandings of this part. They are ready to place the wager to which the preacher invites them in the text for today.

All this ought to terrify the preacher. Those who speak the messages must be driven to seek and enjoy grace. If nothing in their speech or life suggests the beginning of a personal following of these possibilities, we hearers who preach *with* that person have to venture on our own. What could give them confidence if the preacher in no way cares, shows forth, dares, or tries to follow the possibilities?

Instead, the effective preacher comes across a rich set of texts from the Bible, chosen for the observances of the church. Each one of them has been picked apart for decades by historical critics who learned much about the world from which it came. Few texts in the world have been subject to more literary analysis than these in the Bible. Yet because a mother, a high school janitor, a prisoner of war, a teacher, a friend, or a pastor has found disclosed in these a life in a new community and a trustworthy set of custodians of the message, a new generation begins to try on the meanings. Then the texts startle hearers with their freshness. The preacher must move on to the text to do the opening of that possible horizon toward the world of God and of disclosure. Listen for a salutation which makes the people participants:

5. Dear Friends

Why are they dear to this preacher? As a called servant of a congregation, it is probable that members have the messenger on the payroll. If this situation means that the relation of preacher to preached-*with* is one of dependency, then it is all degrading and the word "dear" is phony.

Dear can mean many things, beginning with mere convention. Every guest preacher must experience a feeling of strangeness in the effort to create intimacy through such a device. If people in congregations think about it, they, too, may find it artificial. Who do such guests think they are, coming to preach at strangers when the regular pastor is gone, "dearing" the members? They are not all that dear. They ran their last pastor out on a rail, and have a reputation for being tough, not dear, to preachers. Is this guest trying to receive a call, to become regular by being chummy?

The word "dear" is, of course, a convention and it is not likely that most preachers think much about it when they use it. Yet it is valuable to make more of it. "Dear" includes meanings like "beloved" and "high-priced," two words that pretty well summarize the relation of these people to their God. They have become dear as beloveds, as lovers are—to the point of God's self-giving of divine life in Christ. They are dear as precious, expensive, because that price was high.

Dearly beloved, or dear *friends*. Once again, this term

can imply a feigned intimacy or can be a genuine attempt
to provide a spiritual meaning for the relation. It becomes
clear that if the ensuing sermon is to have effect, both
where it might have to denounce the ways hearers have
chosen to block the path of God and to announce the
ways God has broken through the blocks, this set of
people must be friends. Now the preachers-*with* (with
the message of God) take on new importance. Without
a good group of friends to hear, the speaking cannot have
good effect. When President Lyndon B. Johnson decided
not to run for office again in 1968, Mike Royko wrote
a farewell newspaper column which included two concluding truths: "You," he wrote Johnson, "were not the
best president a people ever had. But, then, we were not
the best people a president ever had." The two somehow
have to experience a common chemistry, to provide a
basis for their agreements and disagreements alike. The
sermonic world differs little from this.

The moment the preachers say, and mean, "beloved,"
or "friend," they have set out to establish a communion
in which the hearer is of full importance. As friends, both
are equals, even if their callings differ somewhat. One
is called to preach, the other to hear and preach-*with*.
Yet both stand in need of grace, both are heirs of the
same gospel.

How does one establish the role of the friend and then
still keep the freedom to open the possibility that God is
displeased with existing modes of believing, thinking,
and acting into which hearers have fallen? How can there
be a proclamation, prophecy, or law among friends? The
answer: easily, or effectively when not easily. One of
the most durable elements in the whole concept of friend-

ship is this: it is precisely the friend who can and must serve to guide another person. Whenever the friend sees someone whose trivial wrongs have begun to grow gross, whose minor deviances have led to delinquency, whose quirks are leading to great outrageousnesses, it is likely to be revealed that this person did not have a profound friend. A friend is someone who possesses position, courage, skill, grace, and care to say, "This time, friend, you went too far." Or: "Friend, that conduct creates an irritation which, if it bothers *me*, must drive your enemies to distraction."

Sometimes with a confirmation class in a small church the pastor may in the midst of a sermon proceed down the line of confirmands and talk not about but to each member of the class. There is risk in this, for at least with a teenage class there is a high chance of embarrassment. The problem can be overcome with no necessary invasion of privacy occurring. In each case a congregant hears a little biography, a lifting out of the mixture of qualities, most of them the better qualities which form the memory-impression or the image of the person to the preacher. In that act these young friends become vivid participants in the sermon. What the congregation hears is not a true or full biography or an assessment of the sort that would come from psychological testing. What results is a gathering of meanings which have come through classes, retreats, recreational periods, encounters during truancy calls in homes. What the pastor offers is the impression of the young person's place in the community, as preacher-*with*, not preached-*to*.

Who are these other friends who make up the congregation? Sociologists tell us ruefully that members of a congregation are more like each other than many would have wished them to be. Some church growth advocates go on to say that modern Christians live and should live by what they call the homogenous unit principle. This principle has discovered that people who are alike seek their likes, also in church. They want to be with their kind, their crowd. Interracial, interethnic, interclass congregations are rare or rarely effective. Congregants rubber stamp and carbon copy each other. That observation may be more true than desirable in the eyes of those who hope that the reconciling circle of Jesus Christ will overcome these differences. It is disturbing to recall that most of the Second Lessons come from epistles in which Paul spent most of his energies trying to get people of difference to live together: Jew, Greek; circumcised, uncircumcised; men, women; eaters of certain meats and non-eaters; rich and poor. Paul often failed, and the preacher today has failed.

Yet if the sociologist and growth expert see the likeness between people, the preacher knows the differences. Do you know yourself? Can you understand your mood today? What about the spouse, parent, child, or person closest to you? Years of familiarity make them only partly predictable to others. People married fifty years know all that seems to matter about their spouses, and then suddenly learn that for all the years this spouse has carried a secret, a burden, a resentment—or faces death in ways completely opposite to those envisioned.

Look around, there is a person who can barely contain herself because she has within the week acquired an M.B.A. degree, a position to go with it, and a loved one with whom to share all. Eucharist or thanksgiving comes so naturally that she may hardly understand how the text for today must give her special reasons why the sacramental bread and wine are part of an enactment of a special Presence. She is a dear friend to the preacher, as is the man two down from her. He is the president of the congregation, a self-assured-looking man, well dressed, educated, polished, accomplished. Yet this week there is a sag in his shoulders. He is part of the same story as Ms. Bright, M.B.A., but what is promise for her is threat for him. His company became part of a conglomerate and he is expendable after mid-career, at the height of his powers. What in the text for today talks to his fear, his loss of dignity?

The preacher knows that the woman four rows back may wish for an unfermented grape juice cup at Eucharist, since she is struggling with alcohol, but has not yet "surrendered," and will not yet be pushed to Alcoholics Anonymous. The preacher also anticipates that this week, as always, there will be a tear in the eye of both in that couple who come warily to the Table. She sheds tears because she has had a mastectomy and he sheds one because shortly before he had wanted to leave her. Now he feels guilt for having the want and fear for what is ahead. Will their shield stay up, or their defenses go down, so that the fright and dread they carry can acquire meaning and that the grace announced and believed in become theirs?

A retarded young man churns in the third row. He is not listed as intelligent, but the preacher knows that the lad knows what the gospel of the Lord is. The speaker of the Word also knows the resentment in the heart of the parents. They all but carry the child to places like

church. Their resentment is often, not always, overcome
by the fire of love opened in the world in front of the
text.

Personality styles and preferences make up this circle
of friends who, by their variety, are making it a lively
challenge to see them as preachers-*with* this day. The
woman sitting over toward the side has what Karl Rahner
calls a "wintry sort of spirituality" and could not wave
her hands above her head and shout "Praise the Lord!"
if the kingdom depended on it. The man next to her has
the summery, sunny sort of spiritual style which suggests
that one should always wave the hands and shout "Praise
the Lord!" because the kingdom depends on it. He does
so with ease and joy.

I have counted to ten in this gathering of a couple
hundred, and pointed to only one aspect of the many
selves they bring each week or in a succession of weeks.
The preacher knows what else is represented out there:
the pro and con nuclear-freeze people; the advocates of
open housing and those who fear for their equity if blacks
threaten to move in next door. One friend has acedia,
which is a sadness in the face of spiritual good. This
week again, though the preacher will fix him in the eye,
there will be no spark. A row behind, someone who is
all spark waiting to be ignited is ready to be carried off
in who knows what direction.

All of the Seven Deadly Sins are present in each and
all the people. Here are the pregnant, the repressed, the
abandoned, the self-abandoned, the promiscuous, those
with secrets, those who have told all the secrets, those
with lifted faces and those with face lifts, those who look
as if they have problems and those who, by not looking
as if they have problems, show that they do. Who else

participates? Those who want to be reached out to during the Kiss of Peace—reached out to? They need to be kissed and would kiss—and those who cringe when nothing more than the Greeting of Peace calls for crisp handshakes and sullen greetings. Those who can stay for coffee hour and those who will covertly make their way away. The saints. The heroes. The louses. There is something of each in all, and though the sociologists type them as all of one kind, they have astonishing sides to show.

One thing each friend has, including those in self-hate stages, is a distinctiveness and, probably, a preference—when challenged—for being themselves. They have to be the raw material for the company of preachers-*with*. They would be changed, they and not some persons they *would* be, until they become in one aspect, at least, the new persons they already are by baptism and faith in Christ. The sermon story is to make them new by faith. Yes, when challenged they know that they have to be the stuff of the communal act which is called a sermon.

Next party play that game in which each person must answer: What person alive today would they rather be than themselves? The first flip round will have them name the rich, the proud, the beautiful, the admired, and the admirable. Then remind them that one must take on all aspects of the life of this other person: the fears, frustrations, bad experiences, threats to their existence, and the like. Soon the point comes where one must add a rule: if you want to play the game you *have* to play the game. You cannot choose to be yourself. You have to choose someone else. When that rule is announced, so many people stop wanting to play that it pays to put on the coffee before they rush for the exits.

The power of a story to address all of them in the name

of biblical events that occurred thousands of years ago is what is astonishing about a sermon. When they do not all want to go where the preacher wants to take them, they naturally can become subjects of their ministers' complaints. Yet Dietrich Bonhoeffer reminded those who preach that their job is not to complain to God about this batch of friends. Instead it is their vocation to represent people, to plead their case, to defend them. They and the people are in this together.

Once upon a time, in the good old days, certainly preachers had better company for preachers-*with* than most of them do today. So must the frustrated ones think, until they see the record of Jesus' disciples in the Gospel of Mark. We have already regarded them as the company of losers. When first I read sermons of Saint Augustine from the fifth century, I pictured them as orations to faithful people who filled arenas as large as the biggest I knew, Chicago's Soldier Field. Those, I thought, were better times when there were more and more decisive friends. Then a biography of Augustine disabused me of such notions. The saint said that he had to break into the theater and bring a few people out almost against their will, frankly against their will, just so he could have some sort of company as hearers. Augustine wrote treatises on God as speaker, spoken, and hearer, but he did so on a much more frail basis than many preachers of today can. In their fewness and weakness the listeners are part of the story we now must tell to know what a congregation is, what preaching and preachers are.

Begin at a different point: *here* follows a reason why the preacher says, can say, "dearly beloved," or "dear friends." Given natural understandings, *nobody should be there*. They did not listen to anyone else's lecture

about the ancient world this week. The great state university down the block has 30,000 students, not thirty of
whom study the religions of the ancient world beyond
Judaism and Christianity. The rest have something else
to do. None of them need be here. In our grandparents'
world they might have had to be present. Aunt Marie
was in the balcony making mental notes of delinquencies
and sharpening her tongue for the Sunday afternoon chas-
tenings she designed to keep the standards of the town
and congregation high and the spirits of the young low.
In our parents' world, when some people stayed put and
when community pressure and status counted, some congregants had to be present for business reasons. Others
would not buy shoes from anyone who did not praise the
Lord. Now people move, frequently. They don't watch
others, they don't care. The reasons to be in church have
to be largely positive: at least, they include good habits
and care for community; more likely, they show a desire
to be "saved" and to be put to work by the story. The
Word has a sharper edge than Aunt Marie's tongue and
offers status higher than that of those who were pros-
perous sellers of goods to church folk.

Preachers-*with* have learned to bring not their sameness
but their variety. Thus they sharpen the preacher's eyes
and broaden the scope of the text. Engaged preachers
who are also true pastors, if they are discreet, have found
ways to make the varied lives part of the sermon. Carefully guarding confidences, these messengers of God need
not reach for books of quotations or snappy sermon start-
ers for illustration. Instead their references will come
from the lives of the real people who participate as preach-
ers-*with*, by what they have said and lived.

Ask any veteran preacher and you will hear them tell

of a common experience. All week long they have been counseling scores of people. Hundreds of events have occurred among the people, some of them involving the pastor. Not a few of these represent crises, turning points in life, great temptations, or triumphs. Now comes the day of worship and the sermon. After the service they hear, "Pastor, thank you for preaching that sermon *just for me!*" The preacher is a bit embarrassed. Yes, the words have been just "for you." You *are* the most important person out there. Yet you were not particularly in mind during sermon preparation time. What had happened is that your ears were open, your antennae were out, your heart was unfolded, you came all in readiness for the message which was designed for *all* the "dear friends." Each brings a horizon that is not fully familiar to the preacher or to the other. That is why the preacher is so busy making the story connect, the text open, the horizons fuse. It goes without saying that a congregation of preach-ers-*with* crowd the front of the church near the speaker. At a distance they are passive, of less help, beyond eye contact, a mass of people and not participants. Picture them united, having visible faces; picture them leaning forward, expectant. Then it is time to see what the preacher-*with* person up front is and is doing in the face of the gospel of the Lord, the text, the Trinity, the friends. For that person is also deeply engaged. That is why so often a sermon may begin something like this:

6. Today, I . . .

Today, I want to tell you the story of the Lost Son. Today, I want to connect the story of Jesus' healing with the circumstances of two of our unnamed members. Today, I want to urge that the text's word of judgment has something to say to our nation. Today, I. . . .

If the preachers-*with* are so important, since the "for you" of the gospel is crucial, then the preachers-*to* also have need to notice. In each of them is a reminder, one which is at once devastating to those who thought that *what* they said was everything, frightening to those who did not care to be in a goldfish bowl, and tantalizing to those who would like to think that who they are and what they do all matters. Effective preachers will know something of all three possibilities of that sentence.

A wise observer of the act of preaching once challenged people to think: Can you recall *five* sermons you have heard through the years? Given time, any of us could put together such a list. Let's see, there was a sermon on our confirmation day . . . and our wedding; I'll never forget the time the bishop installed our pastor and dropped his glasses— how he worked that into the text; and that funny attempt by the minister on our vacation trip who brought the wrong manuscript into the pulpit and didn't find a way for it to match the text. And I remember when the great Reverend Thus preached. And . . . Yes, given time, such a list comes to mind. Yet much time has to be given.

Now, quickly, ask the same person: Can you make a
list of five people through whom the hand of God has
been laid upon you? The five people who through their
Christlikeness drew you to faith and love and hope? It
takes but five seconds to do that; perhaps parents, a spouse,
lover, friend, janitor, great-aunt, or a little child comes
to mind. Often the person will be a preacher. Yes, God
lays a hand on our lives through preachers—but not simply because what they say sticks in memory so long.

This comment does not imply an assault on the intel-
lectual side of their endeavors. Instead it points to the
character of preaching and hearing: that we are usually
fed enough for the day, the week, the season. Then it is
necessary to return. For an analogy so weak that it may
fall apart almost as quickly as one thinks about it: it is
harder to remember the details of five menus at peoples'
homes than to know five chefs or cooks to trust for good
food. The detail of the meal goes to the recesses of the
mind. The quality of those who prepare the meal is what
matters for present and future.

We expect that preachers will speak out of personal
experience, even though it is the Word of God that they
preach. They cannot pass on what is not theirs. If they
have been reached by the gospel, then they can pass it
on. Their burden is heavy (1 Cor. 9:16). Paul knew this:
"Woe to me if I do not preach the gospel!" Yet it must
be not only *the* gospel, but *their* gospel. They preach
also to themselves (1 Cor. 9:23), in Paul's spirit, "that
I may share in its blessings." The goal is that hearers be
"rooted and grounded in love," that they "may have
power to comprehend with all the saints what is the breadth
and length and height and depth, and to know the love

of Christ which surpasses knowledge, that [they] may be filled with all the fulness of God.'' This means that preachers have to depend on God, the God who works on hearers (Phil. 2:13) ''to will and to work for his good pleasure.''

The ''I'' who speaks today needs the circumstances of the day so much that little which happens can be frozen for consumption elsewhere. It is the Lord's Day. Light falls in through the window, across the snow. The people are gathered. This text speaks, and I, called to preach, speak. Some people may leave church saying, ''That ought to be published.'' Maybe it ought to, perhaps in essay form. Some sermons *do* publish well, but in being published change their mode beyond recognition. Most of them do not travel well to print.

For emphasis, let me again recount a personal experience. As a part-time editor of a magazine having to do with *Christian Ministry*, I have long been aware of letters to the editor requesting series by ''the great preachers.'' On occasion editors have gone scouting. They ask religion writers in metropolitan areas: who do the people there find most effective and serious as preachers? Whose sermons should we solicit and publish? Answers come in and, soon, so do requested sermons. Most of them do not seem printable, and, if some are printable and later printed, they tend to rouse readers to ask: ''Is this all there is?'' Alas, the preachers-*with*, who mattered so much, do not come packaged with the sermon. Nor does the person of the ''I'' who ''today'' opens the text.

Then, on the other hand, the editors of such magazines, I included, do some traveling. Repeatedly they will visit with friends who insist, ''Come and hear our preacher,

for a great sermon.'' They come and hear. Yes, it is easy
to see why this preacher at this time in this place is
perfectly appropriate. Yet the sermon will not travel, because the personality is left behind. The written sermon
is not preached well, the preached sermon does not read
well. Even the preacher who writes excellently is very
different from the person who stands between eternity
and time, sacred and secular, chaos and order, scattering
and congregation, and who projects a personality in that
world in front of the text.

Preaching is truth through personality. Phillip Brooks's
famed definition has been repeated so often that it has
become a cliché, and it was probably always at best a
half-truth about some preaching through a few personalities. Yet the grains of half-truth are worth sifting and
preserving. The gospel is not intended to come disem-
bodied; it is about body, divine embodiment in Christ,
in the bread and wine of the Eucharist, in the gathering
where Christ is present among two or three, but not as
a mere idea among ideas.

Preachers-*with* sometimes have difficulty stomaching
a message after they have come to recognize the movement of grace through a personality. For instance, we
have heard on occasion of a preacher whose opinions—
political and theological—do not come close to matching
those of a member of the congregation. Yet that member
is unfailingly a partner in the sermon, not an antagonist.
Why? Something like this: "When my wife died, the
preacher held her hand for the last twenty-four hours.
After she died, it was my hand that was held for the next
twenty-four hours. I'd go if the only exercise in the pulpit
from this person were reading the phone book!'' Not

quite—but there is some element of value in such prior bonding.

It may well be that the opposite situation needs more address if we wish to build up the sense of preaching-*with* someone. What if the preacher does not strike us as a personality through whom truth is reflected, is not vibrant, or capable, or admirable? Those of us fortunate enough to find it easy to participate with our regular preachers often have difficulty imagining what it is to endure weak preaching, really bad preaching, from a weak, really bad person, season after season. In the end, we might fall numb and silent rather than offer advice and therapy across the miles:

● In the end, go to another church?

● Speak to the preacher; is there an awareness of this perception? Is there something that can be changed?

● Are you sure the problem is the preacher, and not you?

● Can the bishop or other leaders move the preacher elsewhere? New starts have often given personalities a new chance. Might another congregation call, since the previous one found the same ineffective preacher capable and attractive?

● Is there any recognition of finitude and an understanding of the act of preaching? This is not a performing art, in which we measure the local fiddler by Isaac Stern, the piano teacher by Vladimir Horowitz, and thus the preacher by a great orator. Great orators usually fail as preachers; great empathizers, sufferers-with, true personalities are better risks as preachers. Are we looking for something that is not promised or expected?

● Can I supply what is lacking in the preaching by

my own preaching-*with* enterprise? That is, can I in this communal context adapt and flesh out a text, converting a half-fulfilling one into something that verges on being satisfying?

• Can I help set up a structure or a circumstance in which we preachers-*with* can, without threat to the ego of the preacher, help work toward improvement? Some parishes use advance study sessions or follow-ups toward this end. In the process, the preaching improves, and the perceptions of critics are broadened to grow more sympathetic.

• Is my restlessness a sign of pride; that is, am I alone having trouble with this personality and the preaching? Have I typed myself as a connoisseur to be satisfied by only this wine, this recording of Scarlatti, this hue of blue? Am I an aesthetic dismisser of all near-miss products?

Having raised all these questions, I am aware that it is not easy to satisfy them with universally applicable answers. Acute problems demand acute solutions. For the vast majority of Christians who draw enough from text and sacrament to endure weak sermons and also for the majority who are nurtured by the preaching, there are other questions to raise when we connect the "I" of the preacher with the substance of what is said.

The fundamental turn comes when the preached-*with* congregation changes its expectation to recognize with Paul that we have this treasure of the gospel "in earthen vessels." The transcendent power of God shines through especially in the weakness of the vessels. We only wish that humans did not so often make it all *that* easy for the transcendent to show because the pots are that clayey! Then can come the building of trust. Lyndon Johnson could not be a great president in part because "we" were not a great people. Walt Whitman said in words that long were bannered on *Poetry* magazine, "To have great poets there must be great audiences." A plain girl stops being plain when she is loved, is graced with a jewel and a gown, and given motives to glow and to transcend her plainness. The ordinary athlete improves when expectations rise, as does the child in school. When a congregation grows with its preacher, the preacher may soon set the pace. There are ways to signal this expectation. What the preachers-*with*, the hearers, have a right to, is the very best the preacher has to offer.

Disciplined ministers of the gospel can develop an ethos in which preachers are not expected to linger at wedding receptions after sundown on the night before a sermon. The people have a right to expect the physical best of this "I", but they may not always have helped guard those nights-before for their preaching-pastor. They can also let the preacher know if a drift toward the casual develops. On a few occasions I have been backstage when one of the great performing artists of the world frets before going on stage. She constantly works her fingers, paces the floor, fools with the violin, or warms up her voice; it is just as well that no one gets near while she works out her nervousness. It is always as if this is her first appearance in public. These people deserve the best.

Sometimes a congregation permits an ethos to develop in which the elders gather in the pastor's study before the sermon and "shoot the breeze." Inefficient church officers pester with details that could be handled any other of 167 hours in a week. The pastor wants to be jocular, and jokes. There is no room, no place for retreat, prayer, quiescence of fears or creative channeling of them, fine tuning, getting up to pitch. In other churches there is provision for these and there we have the preachers at their best.

"Today, I. . . ." And the sermon has begun. The preacher may be reading the manuscript. I risk alienating some preachers, but am emboldened to ask, "Why?" If the week has been given over to back-of-the-mind mulling of the text and if hours have been given to formal study of it, there should be enough ease, combined with art, that an intelligent person could speak, and not read. One wishes for each of them that the manuscript could be lost. They would be forced instead to speak—in order to be free. Ask any set of preached-*with* people whether they prefer literary elegance from a text at the end of the preachers' noses or near-elegance from a text preached eye to eye. The returns will be so one-sided they do not even need be reported with precision. Freedom from the sermon text, whether it has been memorized or created in advance for re-creation later, allows for just such re-creation. The God who creates cosmos out of chaos is present through the Spirit who engenders a spirit of enjoyment. We, the congregation, then find the formulation growing in front of us and hear the precise turns of phrase adapted to our moment and need.

Into that freedom for new formulation, there has gone great care. Franz Kafka once said that for the writer the night is never night enough, the silence never silent enough. So with the sermon preparer. We who would preach-*with*, and who would be the hearers who complement the preaching, have to learn to encourage such night, such silence. To grind up the preaching pastor in chauffeuring activities, ticket selling, or other distractions at which clergy never excel, is to cheat ourselves and people in greater need. To make pastors feel guilty when they are caught reading a book is to steal any possibility of hearing a growth in preaching. To force them to live always-observed, always-judged lives is to repress the freedom out of which good character, Barnabas's qualities, can grow. To expect them to be uninteresting, always noncontroversial, is to limit their power to understand a gospel that is always somehow interesting and may be controversial to someone.

Most important, to deny ministry to speakers is to fail as preachers-*with*. Those who speak the gospel may profit because they hear themselves speaking, but they also need to have the gospel of the Lord lived, conversed, and preached to them. Retreats can help. Yet the I-Thou relation of parish life is the most important place for the good news to be effected. The practice of the presence of God by the people, in disarming, good-humored, not stuffy ways, will also help.

I remember a clue from somewhere in Robert Coles, the Harvard psychiatrist, which led in my mind to a full-scale picture: if a person comes to a sanctuary and there senses the presence of God—through the silence, music, preaching, attitude, or whatever, this presence will be palpable, and you cannot keep people from returning. If the sanctuary does not evoke a sense of that presence, no matter how eloquent the preaching and fine the music, you cannot draw the people back again. Somehow the chemistry of the presence is not easily mixed only one or two hours a week. It develops in the bearing of people to each other, of preachers-*with* to preachers-*to*.

We can rightfully make provision and then expect the preachers to be scholars of the text and participants in the gospel and the presence. It is also then possible to make it easier for them to become scholar-observers of our "world," and thus more interesting to us. This does not, dare not, mean they must overcome all distance. We do not serve preaching well if we expect God's messengers to be the most casual bon vivants and boulevardiers in the parish, the droppers of mildly dirty jokes, strokers of the longest golf balls, threats to no one. They become experts at our world in part by empathy, in part by supplying what we would otherwise have trouble recognizing: discernment.

The preachers-*with* help improve preaching by acts as simple as developing friendship with preachers. Sometimes ministers have been schooled by obsolete seminary customs not to make close friends in the parish. Other clergy are distant, sometimes apparently rival, and often are reproducers of a world with which they are already too familiar. Why should they not have friends in the parish? The friend is the agent of a larger world, the living test of relations, the provider of the stuff out of which preaching grows.

The preacher gets help when those who would be preachers-*with* open their vocational lives. Has the preacher been on an assembly line and seen both the boredom of repetition and the camaraderie at coffee break? Has the one who preaches made the rounds in a squad car, or seen a hospital from the physicians' side of the bed? When the preacher denounces technology, does this come from stereotype or has there been an experience of the computers and laboratories in action? Politics is dirty to the preacher who does not find a chance to be in the arena with members who make zoning decisions, school board choices.

Why should the preacher be an observer at the sidelines? I have a subversive theme for seminary commencements and banquets which urges every minister to do a bit of moonlighting. Each should have some outlet which helps keep them from being the slave of the parish. Yes, preachers are called by or assigned to particular parishes, but this is for the sake and good of the neighborhood and the whole church. If the entire ego structure of the preachers' life is dependent upon effectiveness in the parish, there can only be egotism when they greet successes, or defeat and despair when the compliments do not come and the effects cannot be measured. Let the preacher get some knocks and some strokes from being on a zoning board, leading a Great Books discussion group, taking courses at a university, being a member of a club whose purposes are far from those of the church. Encourage the reading of fiction. All these help make the preacher a representative person ("parson," we are told, comes from this notion), and thus someone whose "I" is on a horizon from which hearers will profit. The preacher comes back from moonlighting or daylighting stored with fresh impulses and ideas to work with in the gathering.

There is the preacher; here is also preachment, the sermon itself. Once again, we can slight this event because the library shelves of books on sermons are already so long. Yet we must mention that from the hearers' angle there are things to watch for. These may not all be forthcoming in all sermons, but if a congregation knows for what to listen and a preacher knows the members are listening for these, the act of preaching the gospel of the Lord is likely to be enhanced.

First, while the opening of the world in front of the

text may be complex and while it may admit many possibilities, the sermon itself will be simple. Rosenstock-
Huessy's word about whole books certainly applies to
homilies, short messages: "One book is about one thing—
at least the good ones are." Whatever glimpses we get
of the world of parables suggest that they were about
"one thing," even if people brought many worlds to
understanding them. The mind is not constructed to put
to work a scattering of ideas. There may be many parts,
many hooks, but the preacher, we must remember, has
been working all week to find the one thing with which
to change us, to send us home.

Second, the sermon will be a dialogue. That may seem
strange to the eyes and ears of those who have seen
attempts at dialogue sermons by two preachers up front.
Maybe these worked, but usually they did not, and the
experiment was then abandoned. Every good sermon is,
however, in its own way, a dialogue. The ordered re-
presenting of the Word does not permit a chaos of voices.
Yet the effective preacher is trying to anticipate our ob-
jections, read our faces, know when a point has been
made, detect some psychological clues and encourage-
ments. Drifting, dozing, passive congregants are of little
help in promoting this effectiveness.

This is the point to give away a secret to congregants.
Guest preachers know congregations better than one would
think. Ask anyone who has been on the road and has
stopped at many sanctuaries. The lore is consistent: you
can always tell, within five minutes, which ones are by
habit listening congregations. It is very difficult to change
one of these on a single occasion or in one season. For
an illustration: years ago I was to speak in the gymnasium

at a Christian high school chapel. Gum-chewing, bored, routine students were marched into the bleachers, a canvas was spread at the center circle, out came a piano and a lectern with a command to preach!

It was Good Friday. One glance at the congregation led to a quick revision of plans. The sermon now began:

"Jesus did not die on the cross. No matter what your preachers have told you, if they said he did, they lied. No, at the last minute he was taken down from the cross, his brother was substituted, and he was spirited off to Japan, where he started a religious group that lives on to our time. . . ."

Needless to say, this differed slightly from the gospel the students regularly received in classrooms at this Christian school. One would have expected some reaction: of bemusement over the new gospel, amusement over a preacher who was trying so hard to be interesting, disgust over such a dumb opening, horror at the blasphemy. I do not recall, however, a missed beat of any gum-chewers, a flicker of a raised eyelid to let me know that any humans were in there behind the lids. I then told them that this was a strange story told by a sect in Japan, announced the Good Friday story, and then headed away with an "Amen."

On other occasions, far more often than we deserve, guest preachers are in congregations whose postures, eyes, bearing, participation in worship, and greeting frighten because they show that they do listen and hear each week. They have been "in training" and are ready for the next contest with the preacher.

A third mark of what to watch for in preaching—and to mention subtly if it is lacking, as it often will be—

comes in a response to this kind of question. "Does the preacher talk about God or offer God?" This was one of "eighteen criteria for effective preaching" which challenged us when I went to seminary under the master teacher to whom this book is dedicated. He would send his classes scurrying to the library to find in printed sermons all eighteen of his chosen signs of effectiveness, but only this one usually stumped us. A lecture talks about God, a sermon offers God. God, says Buber, is addressed (Thou) not expressed (It). As Stählin said, in worship, in the sermon, something happens—it does not *not* happen. God offers what it is to be God: love, life, power, wholeness. To know Christ is to know his benefits. This understanding of enactment, offering, not describing God, has stood me in good stead in measuring the power of sermons ever since. I have never yet found one scoring if it only walked around the attributes of God. Seldom does one fail if it does offer God. Those who would preach-*with* do well to alert the preacher up front to this expectation.

Fourth, is the preacher regarding us in the congregation as preachers-*with*, as baptized people who already are in the way of salvation? Or are we all regarded as outsiders to the divine purpose? Is there only a working on guilt, or are we pointed to the graces and goodness of Christ which have already been allowed to grow in us? Of course, sermons must make room for the public appeal to those who stand outside the scope of grace, but to devote every sermon to them is to deny the need for growth in grace.

Preachers-*with* help the sermon reach themselves when they watch for that time which might be called the "Aha!" moment. When did this text come alive for the preacher?

68175

When was it possible for the commentaries to be closed because the gelling idea had come? There is usually an electric kind of instant at which we can see animation in the face of the preacher, sense a quickening of pace, a feeling that here, now, is the moment to drive the point home. If we show no part in the rhythms of the sermon and greet each minute of it with the same degree of apathy, it is not likely that any but the most tireless preacher will allow any of this animation to show through the seasons.

The sermon is not finished if we are not asked to preach it through our living. Years ago I thought that the following notion might move along the art of preaching. Get people to leave the setting saying not, "That was an inspiring sermon!"

Inspiration quickly wears thin. Instead, second, hope that something connects and they henceforth say, "I never thought of it that way before," because fresh thought does inspire action. Then someone wiser came along and urged a still further goal. "Since I have thought of it that way for a long time, why have I not put the thought into action?"

Here we come to the springs of motivation in the story, the text opened, the world of possibilities presented, God disclosed. Sometimes the motivation grows when Christ is presented for an example, but more often when the love of Christ is seen as controlling, allowing, impelling. Is the given counsel all too vague, or can we be pointed to lives which exemplify something of Christian action? Does this parish have a program through which we can work the works of love, and has it room or can we make room, for us to use it as an instrument? Is there a clue in the one idea of this sermon for us to carry the new consequences into our vocations, whatever they be— including sickbed existence?

To move much beyond clues like these would be to write a book on sermon preaching, not sermon hearing, and preaching-*with*. The minutes quickly pass, as does the attention span. The Eucharist is now waiting celebration. The brown book we mentioned pages ago comes back with a clue once again:

> The Votum ("the peace of God which passeth all understanding. . . ."), which the Common Service of the Lutheran church prescribed at the end of the sermon, was a little benediction which in a sense brought the Liturgy of the Word to a close. In the *Lutheran Book of Worship* order, the Liturgy of the Word continues through the Prayers and so no benediction is appropriate following the sermon. Retaining the Votum would seem to isolate the sermon as a special action separate from the rest of the service. That is a common notion, but one to be guarded against.*

Properly guarded against, then, it remains only to be said, at the end of the preaching:

---

*Philip H. Pfatteicher and Carlos R. Messerli, *Manual on the Liturgy: Lutheran Book of Worship* (Minneapolis: Augsburg Publishing House, 1979), 223.

7. Amen

The preacher and sometimes lively people end the message or respond to it by saying "Amen." Unless we are Jews and even if we are Hebrew-reading seminary graduates, we do not speak much Hebrew. Yet this word "Amen" has entered our vocabulary. We say it at morning and evening prayers, at table grace, and upon concluding the Lord's Prayer. When it concludes the sermon it has a special place and meaning.

"Amen!" does not mean the service is over; even at hillside summer camp vespers and certainly in a house church setting, there is more to come. In the formal services of worship the congregation usually moves to sing the foremost hymn of the day, one which is carefully chosen to reinforce the theme of the sermon. This means that the congregation, in song, remain "preachers-*with*." Now that the gospel has sounded out, the people know how to respond in song, to begin to apply the theme to themselves in new ways, and to testify to each other that they are part of the sermon.

"Amen!" leads both into the hymn and the creed. "We believe," we preachers-*with*: we take on ourselves the meaning of the message. And from the Creed the congregation moves to prayers which continue the theme of "Amen!" Prayers, whether they are to "intercede" and speak up for others or ask God's blessing on human commitments, have a special goal.

British philosophers have spoken of the "performative'' purpose of some language. When language states a fact, the response may be ''Prove it!'' When language says, ''I dedicate this building!'' or ''I announce a holiday!'' we do not say, ''Prove it!'' We begin to use the building or enjoy the holiday, thus letting the language become performance. When the preachers-*with* turn to the ''Amen!'' as a prayer, they are using language which commits them thus to building, or enjoying, or whatever it is to which the message and theme of the day have led them.

''Amen!'' in the gathered service ordinarily leads further into another astonishing version of the Word, the eucharistic meal or the Lord's Supper. It is itself one great ''Amen!'' a very important way of responding to the message. Here Christ is recognized and received in the midst of the people and from this table Christ presently goes out with the people to their daily calling and their common tasks.

Given so much weight in an ''Amen!'' a word which is not so much the end of anything as an escalator, a traffic control movement, an agent to move people to a new stage, we do well to pause for a moment and think of what it means.

Sometimes it is valuable to treat words naively, to take the most common terms to the open dictionary and visit them as if they had never been heard before. So the Oxford English Dictionary, the giant of them all, opens up *Amen* by telling us that it comes from the Hebrew *ā-mēn*, which means ''certainty, truth.'' In the Hebrew Bible it was ''an expression of affirmation''—the congregation, through it, says ''yes''—consent—''we go along''—or ratification—''watch us in action and you will see us performing what we have heard." This is all true even though, as the dictionary reminds us, what we affirm, consent to, or ratify, "has been said by another" (Deut. 27:26; 1 Kings 1:36). Early Christians, says the same dictionary, adopted this address "as a solemn expression of belief, affirmation, consent, concurrence, or ratification of any formal utterance made by a representative." The representative in this case has been God's own, a human deputy, the reacher among us.

To what do we commit ourselves, as preachers-*with* who participate in preaching by living out of the gospel's "Amen!" in the week ahead? Certainly not to all the opinions expressed by the preacher, even though it is impossible to separate all of these from the claims of the Word of God on us. We have demanded that the preacher be concrete, that the message apply to the real world in which we live. Preaching is not about heavens and clouds and ideas beyond our grasp, but about the world of computers, hunger, generosity, lust, warfare, domestic policy.

The preacher has to set forth certain models, give some examples, try something on for size. Yet it is never a part of "Amen!" for all who have heard the message to apply it the same way. That Christians in response to a command of God *must* do something to feed the world and the neighbor is clear. The message empowers them to do this. It says not "you have to love!" but "you are given the freedom to love." This gives them no choice but to respond to the neighbor in need. The preacher may urge that all this means support of this or that legislation, this or that policy. People in the congregation may not always agree with each other or the preacher about a

specific bill in the Congress. They may have a different
view of what is a fulfilling approach to feeding: sending
grain, helping in development, or whatever. The "Amen!"
therefore is a general commitment: *somehow* we will take
part in feeding. We have talked about justice; now we
must and will be just. We have talked about peacemaking;
now we will make peace and be peaceful. We have heard
a message of enabling love; "Amen!" says that we will
in Christ know the power to love.

At this point I have to restrain myself lest this reflection
on "Amen!" turn into a full rehearsal of all that the
gospel of the Lord means, all that it calls us to or empowers us to be. Those are themes for other books. Here
it is urgent that we be economical and stay on the single
point: that people are participants, preachers-*with*. This
means that we can leave the gospel to do its own work,
in hymn, Creed, Eucharist, and living, and ask here and
now only what part the congregation of hearers plays in
the development of the preacher and preaching.

One of the casual but delicate points at which this all
comes up occurs in a kind of liturgy involving "what
happens at the church door," or at lunch after the camp
services, or at dinner in the house church. Think of a
typical formal setting. People file past to shake the
preacher's hand. The New Testament says nothing about
this ritual, but it seems the natural thing to do. With that
handshake can come a simple, "Good day!" For many,
the instinct is to say, "I enjoyed the sermon!" Some
others have read in church periodicals that some preachers
find this line to be too routine and demeaning. "How
can you enjoy a sermon," someone sneered, "if it effectively did what it should—shiver your timbers, quake
your soul, undercut your smug ways. You enjoyed it?"

Well, yes. It is not necessary to be too surgically pure about the greeting. Yes, "Amen!," if the preaching really reached the core of my soul and helped me be pulled loose from all that kept me from God, I "enjoyed" it. Did it lead to repentance? In the Gospels repenting is not a grim, mopey act. The images there are usually very positive: something new is happening. God is present, the kingdom is at hand, the hearers get to see what prophets and kings wished to see, they are like the bridal party in the presence of the groom. "Repent!" Amen, yes, I will. I enjoyed that. And repenting is followed with an announcement of the message, one which does not merely talk about God but which enacts the divine presence, sees that something is not not-happening. Yes, I enjoyed that.

"I enjoyed the sermon!" can become a legitimate code word, one of many in a congregant's repertory, to signal that the message has connected. A Christian heart has been filled and fed, a believer goes out in the joy of the gospel. On other days something more original might be said, but "I enjoyed that!" as a final Amen is not the worst form of bond. It is not unfair to report the secret that ministers of the gospel as humans also welcome strokes. What they have preached about the new creation in Christ is God's great stroke to the congregation. Yet the minister, in hearing the message, still welcomes its confirmation. The ministry can be a burning out activity. Lived at full intensity, it can mean that a preacher is constantly being poured out. It can be a lonely activity. "I enjoyed the message!" is one way of reigniting, re-filling.

Preachers-*with*, however, will find ways, not always at the church door, to signal their participation in improving the act of carrying God's message. The ways to do this are as varied as are personalities. Professor Joseph Sittler, a magnificent preacher, has told about how in his youthful days as a parish minister, he counted on a usually quiet but always present, always honest, aged parishioner to signal what he needed to know. One week his message was very flawed. As she shook his hand she did as much as a course in preaching or a summer retreat would for his improvement, all with one line: "Pastor, it is evident that you've been very, very busy this week." He had been, but not busy enough carrying out the responsibility that went with this message.

There are ways for Amen!-sayers to take the pressure off salty old ladies, spouses of preachers, or crabby carpers on what they think are weak sermons. They can structure response and aid in preparation. This means that they become critics of sermons and preachers. Criticism is a dangerous operation and it needs careful planning. Many a preacher may first suggest need for criticism and then find it hard to live with suggestions when they come. Have you noticed that it is a real blow to egos if people fire away at faults and flaws when there is no context for the firing? Yet when a forum is established with its own ground rules, something more positive can occur.

I will risk a statistical stab. It is likely that nine out of ten preachers would *very much like it* if serious members of the congregation would meet weekly for a sermon preparation class. Joint study of a text will help the minister find what the commentaries overlooked: the ties to the lives of people in the year, the week, almost the hour of preaching. Witness by this advance group will provide hooks into which the message can be locked more readily. There will be more "ears to hear" if the participating people have made suggestions toward the specific message. The criticism, in a sense, comes in advance, before there has been an ego to be clobbered. And the preachers-*with* will have been very direct participants.

Second, preachers-*with* can aid the development of God's messengers by the way they participate *during* the service. Lusty singing of hymns, intensity of silence during meditation in the service, sitting near the speaker, alertness to the readings, all these set up that "revelatory constellation" of which we have spoken. The preacher is more ready then to sense the presence of God, to serve as a spark to connect the Spirit with these lives. The posture—perhaps a slight leaning forward, a face that shows engagement, eyelids which are not shut—is an awesomely important way of saying Amen! Such a posture is not likely or even possible if Christians have had a three-martini 3:00 A.M. evening before the service. If they drag themselves to worship at all, they will not be receptive. People who hear can be agents of better hearing by "going into training," perhaps keeping a kind of vigil on the Sabbath eve.

As for follow-up, there are also many possible devices. The group which meets to plan the next worship can reflect on the past one. We have heard of churches where people stay to converse about the sermon, a half dozen of them reflecting on the hour of worship—and saying it all into a tape recorder only an hour later. In no time they forget that the tape is present and interact freely. The preacher can later listen to it and hear. Years ago a young and cynical sociologist, Peter Berger, came close to home when he said that "the most common delusion . . . is the conviction of ministers that what they preach

on Sunday has a direct influence on what their listeners
do on Monday.'' This conviction, he went on, because
it is so important for the ego and self-image of the preacher,
''is adhered to despite mountains of evidence to the con-
trary.''

Such cynicism may be well-grounded, but it is also
paralyzing. Better to hear what the people thought they
heard and intend to do about a message than to sulk about
how they misunderstand and do not follow. The minister
who hears reports of this sort stands a chance of being
doubly careful in the future choice of words, the shaping
of the message, in the sermon next to come.

To speak of advance training by preachers-*with*, the
posture of alertness, or taped response criticisms as part
of the ''Amen!'' would be to leave the ''ratifying'' all
on the level of words. Peter Berger was on the right track
when he observed negatively what now needs picking up
with the positive. The test of the message and the ''Amen!''
is in the lives lived. The people who heard and believed
did not thereby stop being sinners. They did not get a
lifetime dose of gospel. They did not now have all the
facts on which to act. They had instead been fed for *this*
day, *this* week. They have had the chance to participate
in recognizing the presence of God in the Word of divine
presence. There has been enough nurture to carry them,
fallible mortals, until the next announcement of grace.

A sermon has to move out beyond church. In the nine-
teenth century the Danish philosopher Søren Kierke-
gaard, who knew how to use words to shock, once said
that Martin Luther ''says somewhere in one of his sermons that properly sermons should not be preached in
churches. This he said in a sermon, which surely was

delivered in a church, so that he did not say it seriously. But it is true that sermons should not be preached in churches.'' Yet if they were not preached in churches, there might be even less care about preaching at all, about taking the message seriously. Here a both-and situation is urgent: sermons must *also* be preached, conversed, and lived outside churches.

Some of this enacting also does take the form of speech. Christian *conversation* is an expression of a calling. Believers are ordained by their baptisms to speak to each other and to an uncaring world about what God is doing. Preachers-*with* may very well listen with an ear to taking out their version of the message to which the speaker and they are soon to say ''Amen!'' They adapt the message from the sanctuary into the world of work and parties. Some of them, especially the young, may be moved by preaching to become preachers. Yet most of them, especially those too old to entertain a career in formal ministry, are preachers-*with* by the way they carry the story beyond the gathering. They are so by the way their bodies display the new life of God in Christ in their midst.

Books of morals and ethics can detail what the Christian life as an ''Amen!'' looks like. A little book on the people participating in preaching has to be a celebration of speech, of words, of language. In a world of debased speech, misleading advertising, routine slogans, there is always the chance that preachers-*with* can by their attentiveness join ·with preachers-*to* in realizing once again the ways in which God is present, Christ is incarnate, the Spirit is enflaming, through a spoken message. Martin Luther said that faith was an acoustical affair. A thinker of our time, Eugen Rosenstock-Huessy did not say all that one must say about God, but he pointed to one important way of thinking about God: "The power who puts questions into our mouth and makes us answer them is our God." This God is not an object, but a person, and he has not a concept but a name.

"Nobody can look at God as an object. God looks at us and has looked at us before we open our eyes or our mouths. *He is the power which makes us speak. He puts words of life on our lips.*" If so, the preacher can never be too careful in preparing and delivering the message. The participants, the congregation, the hearers, as people who preach *with* the preacher, can never be too careful in preparing for and hearing the message. They will recognize in what happens that the "words of life" are on human lips. They will live, saying "Amen!"